ABANDONED
NEW MEXICO

ABANDONED NEW MEXICO

GHOST TOWNS, ENDANGERED ARCHITECTURE, AND HIDDEN HISTORY

JOHN M. MULHOUSE

AMERICA
THROUGH TIME®
ADDING COLOR TO AMERICAN HISTORY

America Through Time is an imprint of Fonthill Media LLC
www.through-time.com
office@through-time.com

Published by Arcadia Publishing by arrangement with Fonthill Media LLC
For all general information, please contact Arcadia Publishing:
Telephone: 843-853-2070
Fax: 843-853-0044
E-mail: sales@arcadiapublishing.com
For customer service and orders:
Toll-Free 1-888-313-2665

www.arcadiapublishing.com

First published 2020

Copyright © John M. Mulhouse 2020

ISBN 978-1-63499-234-3

Typeset in Trade Gothic 10pt on 15pt
Printed and bound in England

ACKNOWLEDGEMENTS

My heartfelt gratitude goes to the many people that have shared their wonderful memories and stories, both online and in person, of the places I have visited. I have tried my best to always get the history straight, to tease out every specious detail, but given the wide-ranging nature of this book, I fear some inaccuracies are inevitable. Please know that I did my best. Otherwise, when the legend has become fact, I have tried to print both.

This book would have been impossible without the people that traveled all these many miles with me, making the lonely road so much less so. Thanks to Malcolm Alcala, Stephanie Baker, Amanda Boutz, Beata Certo, Matt Doherty, Nasario García, Nate Gehres, Lisa Hagen-Glynn, Megan Hancock, Roch Hart, Bob Julyan, Matt Kowal, McCormick family, Mulhouse family, Emily Nelson, Kate Nelson, Rob Pangle, David Pike, Don Priola, Jared Robbins, Kat Romero, Ben Specter, Amaris Swann, Jim Thibault, Mitch Walcott, Colleen Wright, and Rich Wright.

Thanks to Betty Williamson for unparalleled hospitality in Pep.

Special thanks to Alexis Harrison and Claude Mathews for assisting with early drafts way above and beyond the call of duty, and to Judith Bowers, Dixie Boyle, Kevin McDevitt, and Craig Springer for their one-of-a-kind expertise. I am greatly indebted.

During the writing of this book, Richard Baron, Mike Friggens, Rina Ouellette, Rebecca Sharitz, and Betsy Thibault left us. I wish they had not, and I dedicate this to them. See you down the road.

To K. With love and gratitude to you and New Mexico.

CONTENTS

The Desert Sands welcomed travelers to Albuquerque for nearly sixty years until destroyed by an arson fire in 2016.

INTRODUCTION

City of Dust was born not as homage to the desert of New Mexico, nor does it reference the decay of ghost towns. In fact, the name I gave to my now seemingly endless project to document collapse, both physical and otherwise, over the last fifteen years arose from the city where it all began—Augusta, Georgia. The thick red dirt of Georgia is legendary, and as I crept through murky swamps and tangled forests searching for forgotten farmsteads and lost swimming holes, my shoes would invariably become coated with that ochre dust. So, Augusta is truly the "City of Dust," the place where, in 2003, I first picked up a disposable plastic 35-mm camera and began trying to capture what I saw and how I felt.

What I felt was just as important as what I saw in my sudden desire to take photographs of abandoned buildings. In the midst of a stretch of bumpy years, I began to feel somewhat like an abandoned building myself, windows broken and occupants vanished, doors hanging off the hinges, perhaps now not much more than a fire hazard. Yet the buildings that looked like that in Augusta were beautiful, stately things, left to fend for themselves in a once-vital downtown that was well into a few decades of steady decline. There were theaters, barber shops, mills, schools, an antebellum grocery store, and the former home of a governor of South Carolina built in 1799. I learned that if you are going to be vacant, you can still be lovely, at-risk, but weathered in a way that hinted at a thousand stories—in a word: alive. I found these places inspirational and consoling, and I began to shoot them by the dozens with no particular thought as to what their stories might actually be or even what I would do with all the pictures.

A couple of years later, when I posted the first photos on the City of Dust blog, I started to research the history of what I had shot and was stunned. When I had visited that antebellum grocery store, I figured it had been built in the 1940s or '50s; I was off by a century. The only thing I knew for sure was that I loved it. A brick ruin across the Savannah River in South Carolina was the site of a club where the woman that was the inspiration for *The Three Faces of Eve* once danced. Every place I had photographed seemed to hold a surprise. I found the pairing of these abandonments with their forgotten tales transformative. The process made me feel hopeful.

I continued photographing in Minnesota, Tennessee, and California, but upon moving to Albuquerque in 2009, I realized I was surrounded by material that stretched as far as the endless horizon, including entire towns. I spent the next nine years criss-crossing the state, researching and photographing, always trying to get farther off a path that had already left the main thoroughfare years ago. This book represents a significant part of that time, including most of what I posted on the City of Dust blog between 2010 and 2017. There are many other locations I wish I could have included in this book, but sometimes even I have to be reasonable.

I hope it is apparent from what I have written above, the way I present the locations below, and the photographs themselves that I have no interest in "ruin porn." My goal is to give every building and town the affection and respect it deserves. Usually people still live in these towns, and even the utterly abandoned was once important to somebody—besides me, I mean. There is also a wider socioeconomic

This home, purchased from the Sears, Roebuck & Co. catalog, belonged to the Ayers family, once prominent in Estancia, NM.

story here—that of farms failing, businesses going under, and the young seeking opportunity in bigger cities. Those melancholy trends continue many decades on not just in New Mexico, but in rural areas across the country.

There is an astounding amount of history hiding in the background of these pictures, too. On any given day in New Mexico, you can find evidence of Ancestral Puebloans, perhaps a potsherd or stone wall, remnants of a vanished culture stretching back well over a thousand years. Or maybe you will see a Navajo pictograph in a remote cave, the work of a painter who passed that way hundreds of years earlier. Juan de Oñate y Salazar, the conquistador, entered what is now New Mexico in 1598, claiming the land for the Spanish Empire, and heralding the beginning of steady trade and migration from Mexico City to San Juan Pueblo just north of Sante Fe. This route would be forever known around the world as *El Camino Real de Tierra Adentro*, "The Royal Road of the Interior Land." While the quest for cities of gold and converts ignited bloody conflict, a unique culture established itself, one that remains wholly identifiable to this day. It would take a couple of hundred years for other Europeans to truly begin to make their way to this rugged land from the east, often themselves in search of those precious yellow rocks.

New Mexico became a territory in 1850, and the ranchers and cowboys arrived in number; the Goodnight-Loving Trail traversed the entirety of the future state from south to north by the 1860s. However, the Land of Enchantment would not officially be part of the union until 1912, only a little over a month ahead of the forty-eighth state, Arizona. The railroad was king by then, but Route 66 was not far off. Less than a decade later, the Dust Bowl blanketed the northeastern corner of New Mexico and, in combination with the Great Depression, led to an exodus from which some areas have never recovered. Then there was the Trinity Test near Alamogordo, the establishment of the interstate highway system, and the diminishing of the precious railroad. All these events and many more can be seen in the periphery of these photographs when not already front and center.

Before we visit the places where the things I have just described occurred, I want to say a word about ghost towns. It is quite rare to find a place wholly uninhabited, a "true" ghost town, and while they exist, they are often not very interesting to visit because usually not much remains. See the chapter on Carthage and its neighbors for the difficulties encountered in visiting 100-percent ghost towns. While not every village or town included here is a ghost by any means (e.g. Encino, Vaughn, Monticello, etc.), I will mention a commonly used definition that considers a ghost town to be a place that has: 1.) Significantly decreased in population from its peak; and 2.) For which the original reason for its existence has disappeared, whether it be gold, steam locomotives, or pinto beans. Given that, I do not believe that anyone

Nara Visa, NM, may fit the broad definition of a ghost town, but that does not mean it cannot have the well-maintained Sacred Heart Catholic Church still holding services.

should feel at all slighted to be a resident of a "ghost town," maybe not even those living in Detroit.

Finally, a large number of the photographs in this book were taken with film spanning a disordered array of stock types and expiration dates, including a couple medium-format shots. I prefer to use film as it keeps me honest, taking as few photos as possible and making them count. I also find my film shots more satisfying, possibly for those reasons, although I am not entirely convinced it is only that. Yet there are photographs taken digitally included here, too. I try to be nothing if not resourceful, using whatever is at hand in my attempts to capture a little bit of my soul in a quiet one-room schoolhouse or lonely gas station. On the rare occasions when I am especially lucky, I hope I might capture something of the souls of those that have gone before me, as well.

1

THE ALBUQUERQUE RAILYARDS

Albuquerque, New Mexico's, largest city, on the banks of the Rio Grande, would not have risen to such prominence without the steam locomotive and the incredible industrial cathedral built to service them.

TRAIN I RIDE: ALBUQUERQUE

The Albuquerque Railyards are a massive complex sprawling across 27.3 acres and sitting (mostly) idle off 2nd St. in the old Barelas neighborhood near downtown Albuquerque. Established by the Atlantic and Pacific (A&P) railroad in 1880 after the city was designated as the division point between the A&P and Santa Fe Railways, the chief function of the complex was to maintain and repair locomotives. Most of the shops and offices were constructed between 1914 and 1924, after the Santa Fe had declared bankruptcy and re-emerged as the Atchison, Topeka and Santa Fe Railway (AT&SF), absorbed the A&P, and gained ownership of the yards. By 1919, one-quarter of Albuquerque's work force was employed at the railyards, and most of the city's commerce owed its existence to the railroad. The railroad remained a major economic force in the city until well after World War II, and some limited operations continued into the 1990s. At present, fourteen buildings remain, mostly clustered in the northern part of the yards; to the south is an operational turntable, built in 1915, which was used to rotate trains as they entered or exited.

Of the buildings constructed between 1914 and 1915, only the thirty-five-stall roundhouse and a storehouse still stand, while buildings for freight car repairs and a powerhouse have been demolished. However, one of the unique things about the Albuquerque Railyards is its state of preservation; virtually every building built from 1916 onward remains, including the flue (1920), boiler (1923), blacksmith (1917),

The Albuquerque Railyards loom over the heart of the city to this day.

The view facing southeast from the roof of the machine shop toward the turntable.

and machine shops (1921), an assembly hall (1922), a firehouse (1920), and a car garage (pre-1931), among others. The railyard's buildings were at the forefront of industrial technology; the 165,000-sq. foot machine shop has been considered comparable to the 1922 Ford Motor Company Glass Plant, which scholar Grant Hildebrand said was "the single factory which carried industrial architecture forward more than any other." The machine shop's two-story traveling cranes, one of which could hoist 250 tons, were incorporated into the structure of the building itself. Further, all rail lines, whether inside or outside buildings, ran north–south while a transfer table (pre-1919) for moving locomotives between buildings ran east–west, as did the overhead cranes. Thus the railyard was sturdy and highly-efficient, with the massive locomotives moved easily from one area to another.

Albuquerque's early designation as a division point was important because it ensured that the most significant railroad activity in the region would be centered in the city, with the next-nearest division points in the state located in Las Vegas (north), Gallup (west), and San Marcial (south). In the late 1800s and early 1900s, a locomotive generally left for a one-way trip of only 100–150 miles in the morning, underwent some basic repairs upon arrival, and then returned later in the day to its home shop for further maintenance. Fire tubes, flues, smoke boxes, and boilers all had to be cleaned daily, and ash residue left behind by incompletely burnt coal needed to be continually removed.

While early locomotives managed 40,000 miles between major repair-work, twentieth-century engines routinely went 400,000 miles, which put them in the shop for a complete overhaul every year or eighteen months. Shops such as those at the Albuquerque Railyards completely dismantled locomotives, painstakingly cleaning each part of the engine, lathing wheels, manufacturing replacement equipment, patching, and mending, then testing and inspecting the entire thing before sending it back out. A well-cared-for engine might have lasted fifteen years, and at its peak, the railyards tore down and rebuilt about forty engines per month.

Following a steady decline through the Depression, the railyards experienced a record-high employment of 1,500 workers during World War II, when the switch from steam to diesel engines was temporarily halted. Once construction of diesel engines resumed, the railyards were still used for repairs, but by the mid-1950s, the massive complex was mostly utilized for maintaining rail lines. The railyards were not much more than a storage facility by the time they were completely shut down in the 1990s. Then, in November 2007, the city of Albuquerque purchased the site with the aim of restoring the grand buildings. Since that time, some TV shows and movies have been shot in the complex, including *Breaking Bad*, *Crash*, and *Terminator Salvation* (which I have heard was responsible for covering the beautiful colored windows in the fake grime which is still visible). Even better, since 2014,

Above: A massive crane is evidence of the heavy lifting once done in the machine shop.

Below: A look up from the floor of the machine shop.

the city has hosted a weekly market every summer in the refurbished blacksmith shop, bringing thousands of people back to what was once the beating heart of Albuquerque. However, most of the complex remains vacant and deteriorating, with a 2018 arson fire not helping matters. As is often the case, restoration does not come cheap, and a lack of funds often derails even the best intentions.

2

CENTRAL NEW MEXICO

F rom life-giving rivers and the ghosts of the pinto bean empire to early mining efforts and an infamous robbery, the historical importance of the middle of the state can be found around every turn of two-lane highway.

Music on the Wind: Guadalupe

Let us walk along the banks of the Río Puerco, northwest of Albuquerque, and explore the history of Guadalupe, New Mexico. This vast, empty landscape, punctuated by mesas, canyons, and volcanic plugs, is one of my favorite areas in the entire state to explore.

The remains of the village—also known as Ojo del Padre—are south of San Luis on County Road 279, which intersects Highway 550 north of San Ysidro. It is remote, requiring a drive of many miles down dirt roads in varying states of maintenance to reach—so much the better then. This now almost-total-ghost town was named for the Virgin of Guadalupe, while its other moniker, Ojo del Padre ("spring of the Father"), referred to a nearby water source. Oddly enough, when a post office was opened in 1898, the name used was "Miller," but no one can remember why; that name lasted until 1905, when the post office became Guadalupe.

The first thing that one notices upon rounding the corner into Guadalupe, aside from majestic Cabezon Peak looming in the distance, is the wonderful two-story adobe building leaning precariously just off the side of the road. Built around 1905, this was the home and store of Juan Córdova, and it is often said there was a dance hall behind it. However, folklorist and former resident Nasario García refers to the lower floor of this ruin as not only a store, but the dance hall itself when the occasion called for it, with Mr. Córdova's family living upstairs. It is hard to argue with someone

Above left: The home and store of Juan Córdova remains Guadalupe's jewel.

Above right: Cabezon Peak presides, as always, over the Río Puerco Valley.

This remote adobe, on the east side of the Río Puerco and built in 1924, was once the home of folklorist Nasario García's paternal grandparents.

that lived there, so perhaps this big adobe, which once had an impressive balcony, served all purposes. However, everyone agrees that the dances at Juan Córdova's were major events. In the 1920s, 350 people lived in the area, mostly farming and raising livestock, and these dances, which began at sundown and could go until 4 a.m., would have been attended by those from far and wide. Jose Tafoya was the accordion player while his brother, Luis, handled the guitar.

Yet by the early 1930s, the Río Puerco Valley, like so many parts of the country, was hit by staggering drought. At least half of the cattle died. Then, around 1938, the log-and-brush dam that captured water from the river for local irrigation gave way. The government said rebuilding the dam was too expensive for federal assistance, and the communities along the Puerco were too impoverished to do it themselves. Throw in the lasting effects of the Great Depression and the lure of employment in larger cities and Guadalupe did not really stand a chance. The school, the post office, and Córdova's store all closed in 1958 as the last family left.

While a lowered water table and generally challenging landscape have kept people from returning to Guadalupe, you may find a couple folks hanging around. In fact, at least two structures are maintained and lived-in now and then, one being the old schoolhouse. It is not wise to go roaming around on private property out here, but if you see anyone nearby, it is worth introducing yourself and stating your business. Guadalupe's few present-day residents are friendly, and you will usually be given permission to take all the photos you want of the ruins on either side of the road, which include other old adobe homes and structures slowly melting back into the landscape.

A TOWN WITH TWO NAMES: RILEY

While Sergio Leone's *The Man with No Name* might feel right at home in the ghost town of Riley, he and the town might not fully understand each other. That is because, unlike Leone's laconic anti-hero, Riley has two names. Even though the isolated enclave along the oft-dry banks of the Rio Salado was already known as Riley when the post office opened in 1890, many old timers still refer to it by its original name of Santa Rita. Settled by Pedro Aragon around 1880, the small colony of homesteaded farms established by Mexican-Americans was soon given the name of a local sheep rancher—"Riley." Perhaps there was some sort of naming conflict among rival livestock factions.

Like many a New Mexican ghost town worth its *salero*, Riley was once a hotbed of mining activity with four active mines pulling coal and manganese out of the dry and dusty earth. By 1897, about 150 people lived in Riley, and there were two stores and a stone school.

Above left: School has been out for a long time in Riley, NM.

Above right: The Santa Rita Church is well-cared for and still hosts a feast day each spring.

While—as happened to so many ghost towns—the mines eventually stopped paying out, it was not that which ultimately caused Riley's demise; Riley went ghost because the water table dropped due to drought and overgrazing, rendering irrigation more than tough and farming a losing proposition. Without mining and farming, there was not much else to keep a body busy. So in 1931, after forty-one years, the post office closed up and that was the end of Riley, or almost.

You see, there is one building that is carefully maintained in Riley: the Santa Rita Church. Each year on May 22, the Feast Day of Santa Rita, those with ties to the old community come back together and a priest says Mass at the little church. There is a picnic afterward. It must really be something to be a part of year after year, decade after decade. Yet even at its most bustling, the priest only stopped in Riley once every four months.

Riley can be accessed by gravel roads from either the north or south. From the north, you start at the non-existent town of Bernardo and loop way out around Ladron (i.e. "Thief") Peak. From the south, you have to drive a good distance through the Cibola National Forest and cross the Rio Salado. Either route takes you through a vast and spectacular landscape.

While it is often said this drive is "easy" by New Mexico off-road standards, both times I have been through were touch and go. The first time, the Rio Salado was almost un-crossable—not because it was running, but because the north bank collapsed. My last trip followed a torrential monsoon, which would have surely made the drive impossible. Luckily, the road became so bad the Army Corps of Engineers had to regrade the entire stretch, preceding us by mere hours—how nice of them.

EMPTY DESKS: CONTRERAS

In Socorro County, New Mexico, tucked off a side road that parallels I-25, not far from a muddy stretch of the Rio Grande, is the little village of Contreras. This was where a man named Matías Contreras once raised cattle and sheep and gave his name to a small community. A post office opened in 1919 but closed in 1935.

Not far south of Contreras is La Joya, the literal end of the road, and a map from 1918 has Contreras as Los Ranchos de la Joya. Centuries before that map was made, in 1598, Juan de Oñate's expedition found a Piro Indian pueblo at present-day La Joya and called it Nueva Sevilleta because the setting reminded the Spanish explorers of Seville, Spain.

These days, to me, the most striking building in Contreras is the old, long-empty school, naturally. I do not know much about it, although I do know that students were attending classes there in the 1930s. So perhaps it is one of the many Works Progress Administration (WPA) structures built in the area around the time of the Great Depression. Nearby Alamillo has a WPA school that became (and might still be) a residence; however, it looks quite different to the school in Contreras.

There used to be a plaque to the right of the school's front doors. I was told it commemorated some local folks involved with the school, but before I could get back to look more closely, it had been removed. I do not think it was truly stolen, though. I have a hunch the plaque was taken for safe-keeping because the building is in such poor condition.

Above left: The old school proudly announces arrival in Contreras, NM.

Above right: Every March, the charming San Jose Catholic Church holds a fiesta.

Otherwise, the San Jose Catholic Church, part of Our Lady of Sorrows Parish, is fresh and tidy and hosts a fiesta every March. There are no going commercial concerns in Contreras, but there are some well-kept homes and, if you visit while under the vengeful eye of the relentless sun on a parched, triple-digit day, plenty of dust. Since a semi-ghost town in the Chihuahuan Desert is not a bad place for connoisseurs of dust, everything is as it should be when I am in Contreras, New Mexico.

Too Small to be a Village, Not Large Enough to be a Town: Center Point

On Highway 55, almost 20 miles south of Mountainair, New Mexico, is a lonely and charming old schoolhouse, among the very first buildings I ever photographed in the state. It is one of those abandoned places that are a sheer pleasure to visit, but where exactly are you when you are at this school? For many years, it was a mystery to me as I could find no record of anything besides pinto beans existing in the area. Enter the internet. After a few photos of the school showed up on ghost town and history-related Facebook pages, the story of this little dot on the map, which, it turns out, was known as Center Point, finally came to light.

Center Point is not in Robert Julyan's comprehensive *The Place Names of New Mexico*, but I can still tell you how it got its name because it is smack dab in the middle of the state, right by Center Point Hill. Aside from (apparently) the prohibitively rare and expensive *History of Torrance County*, one obscure mention of Center Point occurs in Bert Herrman's *Mountainair, N.M., Centennial History, 1903–2003* (published by Mountainair Public Schools), which includes Center Point in a list of area schools:

> Many rural schools were three-month terms and began after New Mexico became a state in January 1912. Teacher's salary was $25 a month. Many of the teachers were 16 or 17 years old; they boarded at homes until small teacherages could be built for them. Dozens of schools dotted the countryside as the region developed. There was Eastview, Center Point, Piñon, Round Top, Ewing, Cedarvale, to name just a few. Typically, each had one room and one teacher that taught grades one through eight. The teachers often lived in shacks next to the schools.

According to accounts from 1916-1917 in the *Mountainair Independent*, the school was built on land donated by homesteader William C. Harrison and constructed with the help of men from the community. It most likely opened for classes in 1916 and was closed by 1949, after which time students were bussed to nearby Gran Quivira. However, by then, the area was sparsely populated indeed, and even the

Above left: Lonely Highway 55 will take you past Center Point, NM, in an instant.

Above right: Some of the graffiti in the school has been left by former students.

school in Gran Quivira closed a short time later, possibly as early as 1950. Sadly, Mr. Fulfer was killed in 1935 when a team of mules he was driving bolted and crashed into a gate on his ranch.

I also received a wonderful account from Judith E. Bowers, who spent a short time in Center Point when very young, and provided the most personal written recollection of a life there that I have seen:

My mother, Florence Drew Tausworthe, taught in that schoolhouse. My brother and I went to school there. We lived in a shack across the street. When it snowed we would wake up with snow on our beds. This was in 1946–1947. There was a cistern where we got our water. We had a pot-bellied stove in the house. The people lived on their farms and brought their kids to the school.

My mom taught all the grades. There was a wood stove in the schoolhouse and my brother would go over every morning and light a fire. There were three of us. My oldest brother went to school in Mountainair. It was his job to chop the wood. The wood was brought in by the people that lived in the area. My uncle was the preacher in Mountainair so he would come get us once in a while and take my mom grocery shopping as we had no car.

I thought it was the most wonderful time in my life, but my brothers felt differently because of the hard work they had to do. Oh yes, I forgot, there was an outhouse. I don't know when the school was abandoned as we moved to Willard the next year. I was quite young. We had enough kids for a baseball team. As you are standing looking at the school, to the back left was where we played baseball. My mom was quite brave to live out there with us three kids.

There were cracks in the walls and ceiling of our house and the wind, snow, or rain would come through. We had to use pots and pans to catch the rain. We had a rain barrel also and we used the water to wash our hair. Mama would heat water on the stove for us to take baths in the washtub. We had a chamber pot which my brother had to empty every morning. Being the youngest, I never had to do anything.

We had no toys, so we went wandering. My brother says he got lost one time and it took him quite a while to find his way home. We looked for bird's eggs in the piñon trees. We ate a lot of beans. I do remember buying margarine and mixing the yellow packet that came with it. Mother made a lot of corn bread, so cornbread and beans was our main meal.

When I said I had no toys, it made me remember. My Aunt Leta Hood cut pictures out of magazines for me. They were my paper dolls. I also had some jacks. I was a whiz at jacks. My mama would get down on the floor and play with me. Years later, when my daughter was that same age and we went to visit my mama, she got down on the floor and played jacks with my daughter.

So many people had it much harder that we did, but, fortunately for me and my brothers, we had a very determined mother. So, to me, this story is about my mother, who was determined to be a teacher. She's the one who brought her three children from Texas to New Mexico. And she's the one who probably gave those children in Center Point one of their most memorable school years, as she loved teaching and she loved children.

That was how life could sometimes be in the middle of the last century, right in the middle of the state of New Mexico.

Most of what remains of Center Point can be found at the school.

Pinto Beans and Singing Conventions: Claunch

Travelling south down Highway 55 from Mountainair, past Center Point, following the road through a few sharp turns, one will eventually arrive at Claunch, about 40 miles away. Claunch's position in central New Mexico put it firmly within the pinto bean empire of the early part of the twentieth century, when Mountainair was proclaiming itself the "Pinto Bean Capital of the World," and soldiers fighting in World War I were eating beans that had been grown in the wide open Estancia Valley.

Back around 1900, when Claunch started being more generally settled, it was not known as Claunch. Instead, it was called Fairview, and in the 1890s as DuBois Flats, after local cattle and sheep rancher Frank DuBois. Claunch became Claunch near 1930, when the town was big enough to warrant its own post office and a new moniker was needed. L. H. Claunch, who ran the nearby Claunch Cattle Co., agreed that his surname could be used for the town. Later, he would firmly refuse to let his name be attached to the Claunch Saloon, which therefore never opened.

Claunch flourished in the 1910s and 1920s, before it was Claunch. However, just as Claunch received its name and post office, the Great Depression and relentless drought of the Dust Bowl began to hit Estancia Valley farmers hard. Within a few years, a WPA school would be built, but as more topsoil was carried off by the howling prairie winds, it was already becoming too late. The school closed in the 1950s, but its skeleton rests yet on the plains.

Where it has been said there was once a homestead on every 640-acre section, by the late 1960s, it was more like one homestead for every twenty sections, and only six or eight close-knit families inhabited Claunch. These are numbers that have not increased in the last fifty years, and the place remains isolated, the nearest towns, as ever, being Mountainair and Carrizozo, 42 miles southeast.

While Claunch is largely quiet these days, if you listen closely, you might hear voices on the breeze as singing once echoed loudly across the gravel roads. At first, there were gatherings in people's homes, but then, in 1916, under a brush arbor not far off from town, the Torrance County Singing Convention was born. These were not informal get-togethers, but true events rooted in long religious tradition stretching back to the remote forests of New England in the 1700s. Ralph Looney, relating his attendance at a convention in Claunch in *Haunted Highways*, describes learning shape-notes, a tool for those who cannot read music. Shape-notes have a rich history in a unique type of hymn singing that is considered the oldest surviving American musical form, known as "Sacred Harp" and long-nurtured in the Deep South.

The Torrance County Singing Convention attracted people from all over the region and even those from other states who had moved away. A yearly state-wide

Above left: Highway 55 has claimed another victim in Claunch, NM.

Above right: While the school in Claunch closed in the 1950s, children have played here more recently.

The Claunch Women's Club, established in 1940, is still active.

convention could bring in as many as 1,200 singers. In Claunch, the singing convention year began on the fourth Sunday in April, with other conventions held in June, August, and October; as with Sacred Harp "sings" in the South, food—and lots of it—was required to sustain hours upon hours of music in which everyone participated. After singing through the morning, it was time for a big lunch.

Ralph Looney describes a spread he saw in the mid-1960s, years after one might have assumed Claunch was forgotten:

> Meat loaf, fried chicken, roast chicken, ham, beef roast and pork roast. Turkey, molded fruit salads, slaw, tossed salads. Vegetables like pickled beets, green beans, wax beans, mashed potatoes, potato salad, candied yams. Homemade yeast rolls and cornbread. Chocolate cake, angel food, vanilla cake, white cake, apple pie, cherry pie, blueberry pie and so on and on and on and on." Then would follow at least another three hours of songs such as "Joy is Coming," "Then We'll be Happy," and "When the Roll is Called Up Yonder."

I have been assured there is still fine music being made in Claunch, if not quite on so grand a scale. The post office is also open and operating as a library, too; you can check a book out or swap for one of your own. Walking past the old pinto bean elevator, with "Ye Olde Dance Hall" still faintly visible on the front, and a sign for a museum that looks unlikely to open anytime soon, the past feels more real than the present. The quiet is remarkably soothing, which is not always the case in such places; perhaps it is because the lives that have passed through this place seem somehow still present and singing.

It is worth adding a short postscript regarding Claunch, which lies about 40 miles northeast of the Trinity Site as the crow flies. Given prevailing winds on the morning of the world's first atomic bomb blast, it was directly in the path of potential fallout. People from the region still talk of cows that turned white after the explosion and

The old pinto bean elevator was once repurposed as Ye Olde Dance Hall.

were then shown off at local fairs as curiosities to wonder over. Yet it is cancer that may be the longest-lasting local legacy of Trinity, and while a group calling themselves the Tularosa Basin Downwinders Consortium has spent years fighting for recognition and compensation, it is surely too late for Claunch as the population is now under ten, the old-timers are gone, and their families scattered long ago. It is a strange and unsettling chapter in the history of the soothing little town of pinto beans and singing conventions.

No Rattlesnakes or Pinto Beans: Cedarvale

Let us add another piece to the picture of a region that in the 1920s was the country's largest producer of pinto beans. While you probably are not going to drive through without reason, as you might Mountainair, nor are you going to find it in most ghost town guides, as you will Claunch, Cedarvale was an important dry land farming and ranching community from the time of its establishment in 1908 until the Dust Bowl and Great Depression—along with overgrazing and farm consolidation—forced many of its residents to once again seek their fortunes elsewhere.

It was Ed Smith, William Taylor, and Oliver P. DeWolfe who chose the site for Cedarvale and requested that it be surveyed by the U.S. government. The town would be along the route of the New Mexico Central Railroad, lots were sold through the General Land Office, and a post office was soon opened. The new place was named Cedarvale after Cedar Vale, a town in Kansas from which the founders hailed, and was also located in a valley with "cedars" (i.e. junipers).

Soon, hundreds of homesteaders from other states arrived on "immigrant trains," following the lead of Smith, Taylor, and DeWolfe. Most were looking to plant pinto beans. The relatively high altitude (6,384 feet above sea level) and short growing season of central New Mexico were good for the beans, which could be dry farmed and were in demand, particularly once World War I began and pinto beans were used to feed soldiers. Come fall, the harvest was stored in Cedarvale's three elevators.

The population of Cedarvale would eventually reach about 500. It is now perhaps half that, and there are no functioning commercial operations. The post office closed in 1990. Yet what impresses most as you approach from the northwest along Highway 42 is the looming wreckage of the Cedarvale School. Initially, the school in Cedarvale was a typical one-room affair, but as both the town and Torrance County grew, more space was needed. So, Oliver DeWolfe donated 20 acres of land, and on August 25, 1917, the Torrance County Board of Education approved a bond issuance in the amount of $5,000 to construct a new school.

Above left: The Cedarvale School provides lessons not often found in classrooms.

Above right: A few more seasons of strong winds will surely bring the Cedarvale School to the ground.

The school was finished in 1921 and construction of a gymnasium begun in 1935 by the WPA. By then, the building seems like it would have already been surprisingly big for the area, containing four large classrooms, each of which contained three grades and about fifty students. Children attended kindergarten through to eighth grade and were then driven in the back of a truck a few miles southeast to Corona for high school.

Aside from receiving continuous and dire warnings about a rattlesnake infestation, this massive gymnasium remains the most striking feature of the Cedarvale School. It was surely a gathering place for the entire community, as well as a basketball court (complete with raw wooden backboards still in place) and, judging from the design, probably a theater. I have heard it hosted some bingo games, too. Despite taking the warnings fairly seriously—signs are even painted on the walls of the school—no rattlesnakes were encountered on my visits.

The school closed in 1953 and is now falling down quickly, the years finally overcoming its sturdy construction. The large wooden beams are impressive, and I am told the Cedarvale train depot was built to the same hardy specifications. The depot no longer stands, but the materials were repurposed and used in a home in Albuquerque owned by the daughter of a man who helped build both the depot and the school. I am pleased to have once walked around on that historic lumber.

There are still many people with fond memories of growing up in Cedarvale, as is true for virtually all the small central New Mexico towns where the trains once rattled through constantly and the whoosh of pinto beans pouring from the elevator

Above left: The basketball backboards persist in this terrifyingly decayed adobe-walled gymnasium.

Above right: Despite many warnings, the author has never seen a snake in Cedarvale.

heralded the end of one season and the approach of the next. These are sounds that may yet perhaps be heard, if only faintly, in the startling quiet of pinto bean ghosts like Cedarvale.

THE LAST HANGING CRIME: DURAN

Every once in a great while, I will tell the tale of a ghost town in New Mexico that did not owe its existence to the railroad or mines, whose citizen's livelihoods were not later subject to the capricious placement of state and federal highways, and which did not finally find itself cut off from the travelers that were its very lifeblood. Yet that is not the story of Duran.

In February 1902, the El Paso & Northeastern Railroad finished the "Arrow Route," a stretch of track between El Paso and Santa Rosa, where a connection to Leadbelly's Rock Island Line awaited. Brothers Blas and Espiridón Durán owned wells in central New Mexico, which could provide water to railroad work crews. So the railroad built repair shops and even a wooden roundhouse in what became Duran. The railroad also turned the town into an important supply point for area ranches virtually overnight. Duran's population probably peaked shortly afterward at 300 or so.

However, the railroad eventually moved its operations south to Carrizozo, and the roundhouse came down in 1921. Yet Duran remained vital to ranchers, and when

William Hindi opened his store in Duran, NM, in 1908.

two-lane U.S. Highway 54 came right through the heart of town in the 1930s, the increased flow of north–south traffic gave Duran another boost. This lasted until the 1960s, when I-25 was constructed about 60 miles west, strangling U.S. 54.

Duran is not a true ghost town. It still has residents—probably around thirty-five—but two of its most interesting buildings are long-abandoned. One is a two-story building made of buff-colored sandstone marbled with white. This was a general store and hotel. Badly faded lettering above the doors reads: "dry goods furniture hardware grocery & feeds." It is still a beautiful building whose quaint façade belies a sinister and surprising history.

The building was owned by Anton J. Coury, a man of Lebanese descent, who lived with his wife, Raffa, and their children, Fred, Anna, and Emma, in the upstairs hotel. The story goes that on September 3, 1921, the store was robbed by five men, and Mr. Coury was shot and killed while resisting. Raffa was also shot and severely wounded, reportedly surviving only because a potentially lethal bullet struck the metal clasps of her corset and was deflected. Young Freddy then bravely intervened, driving away the thieves by relentlessly pelting them with canned goods when their gun jammed. I do not know if the store ever opened for business again.

A search for the killers began immediately, and Francisco Vaisa, Isodoro Miranda, and Carlos Rentenería were quickly caught. Luis Medrano was apprehended some months later. The fifth man, Eziquel Machucha, was never found and is believed to have escaped back into Mexico.

The prisoners were sentenced to be hanged on July 28, 1922, but Vaisa appealed his conviction and bought himself some time. On the appointed day, about 40 miles northwest in Estancia, with Mrs. Coury and her children observing, the other

Anton J. Coury's mercantile and hotel, where he was murdered in 1921.

three men were brought to the scaffold as the sun rose. Asked for final statements, Rentenería said a few unrecorded words and Medrano said nothing. However, Miranda said, "In New Mexico, there is no justice for the poor man. He is led like a helpless lamb through the courts and to his punishment. This is an injustice you are now doing." Then, Sheriff John Block led the men behind a canvas drape, the low sun casting stark silhouettes against the fabric. The day broke in earnest as the men dropped to their deaths.

It did not take long for Vaisa's conviction to be upheld, and on April 6, 1923, he, too, was brought to the gallows in Estancia. With few observers and after offering that he had no final statement to make, John Block adjusted Vaisa's noose, the trap door opened, and Vaisa fell as the sun again crested the horizon. He was the seventy-fifth and last person to be legally hanged in New Mexico.

Now, I prefer to get my facts straight, which is sometimes difficult with the internet around. The more commonly cited version of the above story includes four robbers striking in the dead of night, with three men being hanged and the fourth getting the electric chair. Also, the robbery occurred in 1914. While I was not there myself, the story I recounted is the one told in *Myth of the Hanging Tree: Stories of Crime and Punishment in Territorial New Mexico* by former New Mexico State Historian Robert J. Torrez, who references contemporaneous editions of the *Estancia News-Herald* and seems pretty reliable to me.

William Hindi was also from Lebanon and opened a store in Duran in 1908. It too is constructed of cut stone, and its signage still clearly welcomes tourists. Yet much in the world has moved on while the little store has stood still. At least the graffiti inside, some of which reads, "go hug someone," "god rox," and "satan is gay," would lead one to envision a history far more whimsical than that of the

The inside of the Wm. Hindi Store features non-threatening graffiti such as "go hug someone."

general store. William's brother, Kasim, also operated a store, across the highway from the Coury Mercantile Co.

Other buildings around Duran are still in use, including the San Juan Bautista Catholic Church, built in 1910. A red-brick school, which closed in 1955, is now a community center. There is also a fire station and post office. Thus, unlike some other towns where the trains now whistle right past and motorists are few and far between, Duran persists. It also most certainly sees fewer hanging crimes.

THE ROOTS OF PARIS HILTON: SAN ANTONIO

Around the turn of the twentieth century, a boy would walk from his father's mercantile store—which also served as a hotel—to the train depot, just a short distance away. This boy then carried the luggage of passengers newly arrived in San Antonio, New Mexico, back to their rooms, which ran $2.50 a day, including meals. The boy met every train stopping in town, regardless of time or weather. In 1919, that boy, Conrad Hilton, now thirty-two years old, bought the Mobley Hotel in Cisco, Texas, and there began the Hilton Hotels chain; Paris Hilton is his great-granddaughter.

San Antonio can trace its "recent" history back to 1629 and the founding of the San Antonio de Senecú Mission. The Apaches succeeded in destroying the mission in 1675, and for over 100 years, the burnt remains of the village, which had been inhabited by Piro Indians for a mere 700 years prior, slowly decayed out on the plains, a caution to passing travelers on *El Camino Real*. Now those ruins have been fully reclaimed by the desert, and the exact location of San Antonio de Senecú is unknown.

Above left: The train depot was once one of the most important places in San Antonio, NM.

Above right: All that remains on the site where the Hilton Hotel chain got its start.

Some graffiti from over a century ago is visible inside the depot.

Hispanic farmers from northern New Mexico established present-day San Antonio in 1820, and when the Santa Fe Railroad arrived in 1880, the town shifted to be closer to the rails. While most of San Antonio's 1,250 residents still raised livestock, made wine, or even kept bees, the railroad was soon extended 10 miles east to reach the coal mines of Carthage and Tokay. Stakes there included a claim known as the Hilton Mine, owned by A. H. "Gus" Hilton, who used the money to found the A. H. Hilton Mercantile Store. Mr. Hilton's son, Conrad, was born on Christmas Day 1887.

For almost fifty years, the mines paid out, the trains came and went, and stage-coaches ran between White Oaks, Fort Stanton, and Lincoln. However, by 1925, the mines were going bust and the railroad soon took up its tracks. Then two major floods in 1929 washed away a big chunk of San Antonio and the surrounding farmland. World War II lured away most remaining young men and A. H. Hilton's original mercantile burnt around the same time, which, incidentally, pretty much coincided with Conrad's marriage to Zsa Zsa Gabor. However, Hilton's wooden bar was saved and installed in the famous Owl Bar and Restaurant in 1945, where it is used to this day to hold up Tecates and green chile cheeseburgers. The Owl Bar itself was built by the Brunswick Balke Collender Company; you might have used their bowling balls.

That is largely where San Antonio is at today following another move to the north to be closer to U.S. 380, where most business is now conducted. Not a true ghost town, you still will not find any trains stopping at the marooned and precariously propped depot. Crumbling concrete foundations, located across from the old post office (now a restored private residence), are all that remains of the meekest beginnings of one of the greatest hotel chains in the world, without which Paris Hilton might be living in a trailer out in the Socorro County desert.

I Don't Know Where I Am: Carthage, Tokay, and Frailey

Three towns closely linked to San Antonio, New Mexico—Carthage, Tokay, and Frailey—have sunk deep into oblivion. In fact, even the true spelling of "Frailey" has been lost. You might see it referred to as "Fraley" or "Farlay," and either might be right. One spelling that is probably not correct is the one found on the NM Historic Marker beside nearby Highway 380, which has it as "Farley."

Carthage was the site of the first coal mine in the state—the Government Mine—which employed U.S. Army soldiers in the early 1860s and supplied Forts Bayard, Selden, and Stanton. Construction of a railway to ship coal to San Antonio from Carthage began on March 1 of the year that seems to represent the mythological

It is hard to know what's what where three ghost towns blur together.

zenith of the Wild West—1881—when Billy the Kid died and there was a gunfight at the O.K. Corral.

The Santa Fe Railroad Co. finished a bridge across the Rio Grande in 1883, and by 1889, Carthage topped the list of coal camps in the state with a population of about 300. However, by 1893, coal production was lagging, so the Santa Fe Railroad Co. made a deal to move the entire town to Cerrillos, NM. On August 17, 1893, the Old Abe Eagle reported:

> … All the dwelling houses, coal chutes and machinery have already been moved. The place has practically been razed to the earth and the depot, adobe hotel and Gross, Blackwell and Co. are about all that remain.

The Santa Fe Railroad then promptly went into receivership on Christmas Eve. Almost two years later, it would re-emerge as the famous Atchison, Topeka, and Santa Fe (AT&SF).

From 1894, coal extraction continued while mines changed hands and changed hands again. The old Santa Fe Railroad Co. line finally ceased operating entirely in

An unidentifiable ruin in an unidentifiable place.

1896, and then everyone spent some years trying to figure out how to get the railroad to run those 10 miles to San Antonio again. The difficulties of (re)building the short spur came to a head in 1905 when competing mining and railroad interests sued each other. Mining ceased for two years during the litigating. Finally, the case was settled out of court—fifty new miner's homes were quickly built by the Carthage Coal Company, and production surged.

Then, on New Year's Eve 1907, there was a massive explosion in the Bernal Mine, which killed nine miners, throwing two 300 yards from the site. Two more were seriously injured. It was said that many more would have been killed if it were not for the fact that the accident occurred during lunch and most men were eating. A somewhat lesser disaster struck Carthage on February 22, 1918, when coal dust ignited in the Government Mine, killing one mine inspector who improperly used his safety equipment and associated sparrow.

Mining continued for decades, but finally with diminishing returns. The last train left Carthage on August 28, 1931. After that, things were really on the downswing, although serious mining interests struggled through into the 1940s. The last mine, Tres Hermanos, was opened in 1980 by Cactus Industries. It was closed by 1981.

If you look at the entry for Carthage on ghosttowns.com, you will see a note dated April 2, 2000, which laments that most of what had remained of Carthage— apparently a fair amount—had recently been hauled off to a nearby dump. The "clean-up" was ostensibly part of a "desert restoration project," and while I sure love the desert, I find this a little hard to accept. There is so much wide-open space in every direction out here that restoring this small area strikes me as odd—not impossible though, I guess. On the other hand, James and Barbara Sherman's *Ghost Towns and Mining Camps of New Mexico* stated in 1975 that "Today what is left of Carthage is fast melting into oblivion."

Other than the impressive adobe ruins of the large home of mine superintendent John Hart, who left Carthage in the mid-1940s, I have no idea what else has really been lost in the interim.

Whether Carthage disappeared recently or long ago, what remains now is hard to identify. Millions of pieces of broken glass glitter in the sun, many of them pink and purple and thereby showing their age—so much for a restoration. A few stone foundations can be seen here and there. Several old mines can be located, all sealed and capped. Walking the raised rail trestle from the relatively intact Carthage Cemetery, it is unclear where Carthage becomes Frailey, once the location of a limestone quarry and kilns owned by Mr. J. B. Frailey, formerly the trainmaster at San Marcial, another ghostly town along the Rio Grande.

Then there is Tokay, founded in 1918 by Bartley Hoyt Kinney, Sr., who was involved in the Carthage mines and organized the San Antonio New Mexico Coal Company. He wanted to name the town "Kinney," but the post office refused. Finally, while talking to the postal inspector at his general store, he saw a box of Tokay grapes and said, "How about Tokay?"

The Carthage Cemetery is the only easily located feature in a once-active cluster of towns.

Tokay actually struggled into the late 1940s, but eventually mining ceased and its structures were moved to Socorro. It would have been out here somewhere, but no one knows quite where anymore. Just a few miles southeast is the Trinity Test Site, where on July 16, 1945, the first atomic bomb was detonated. Carthage, Tokay, and Frailey, once sizable and active places, could not be much more obliterated if they had been at ground zero.

ANGRY DOGS AND WELL-KEPT GRAVES: SAN PEDRO

There are two ghost towns by the name of San Pedro in New Mexico. One is a former gold mining town to the north, in Santa Fe County, but since we are roaming around U.S. Highway 380 in the central part of the state, we will check out the one in Socorro County.

When Philip Varney visited San Pedro in the late 1970s while writing his book on the state's ghost towns, he saw more than a dozen buildings, including the wood and adobe San Pedro Catholic Church (complete with intact steeple), a school, and another large adobe structure—once the residence of a well-known landowner. Things have changed a bit over the last forty years, and while not exactly a booming metropolis, San Pedro is a little livelier than when Varney came through.

While there might be more actual residents these days (and perhaps meaner dogs, as well), there seems to be fewer buildings. The church is nowhere to be found, nor is the neighboring barbershop. The stately adobe residence has mostly sunk into the earth (and is guarded by one or two of the aforementioned pups). The schoolhouse still remains though. Built by the WPA in 1936, it closed shortly thereafter and is now owned by the family living next to it. They were kind enough to let me take a photo after finding me standing in their driveway when they came home one evening.

San Pedro was settled in the mid-1800s by two families, the Montoyas and the Tefoyas. By 1860, the town had a population of 223, more or less. At that time, the village, located on the east bank of the Rio Grande, was a Spanish agricultural settlement known especially for its grapes. These grapes were crushed, turned into wine, and reportedly shipped "all the way to Kansas." The village was also a resting place and trading center for travelers on *El Camino Real*. Later, some residents became miners and worked in nearby Carthage and Tokay. Apparently, a heated baseball rivalry developed between the San Pedro and Tokay teams with a third community, Bosquecito, also in the mix.

As it was for so many towns, the Rio Grande was San Pedro's lifeblood, and the reason for its location. It was also, finally, a major reason for its decline. All that remains of the section of the river that used to pass beside San Pedro is a dry, sandy

Above: Another of New Mexico's empty schools stands silently in San Pedro.

Below: San Pedro's "windswept and desolate" cemetery.

bed—the result of canals that have shifted the course of the legendary waterway almost 1 mile to the west.

Varney described the San Pedro Cemetery as "windswept and desolate." I love a nice windswept and desolate cemetery, but the San Pedro cemetery, too, has been modernized. A comparison of grave markers shows them to have been upgraded sometime over the last forty years. I will not dare complain.

3

U.S. HIGHWAY 60

To my mind, U.S. Highway 60 is New Mexico's premier road of ghosts. Many of these towns owe both their lives and their deaths to the Atchison, Topeka and Santa Fe Railroad and its construction of the Belen Cutoff through this relatively flat part of the state. Also along this route is Fort Sumner, where Billy the Kid and Sheriff Pat Garrett met for one last time.

A Tale of Three Lucy's: Lucy

Just a little bit east of Mountainair, on wonderfully desolate Highway 60, is the ghost town of Lucy, New Mexico. Lucy is on the south side of the highway, tucked back behind the railroad tracks, so you could drive past day-after-day and never even know it is there.

There are three versions of how Lucy got its name. No one knows which is really correct, but they all involve the railroad. The first is that Lucy was named for the wife of James Dunn, chief engineer of the AT&SF. The second is that it was named after the mother of an attorney for the AT&SF. The third is that the town's namesake is Lucy Myers, daughter of railroad construction engineer Frank Myers. Maybe they are all true. Oddly enough, despite these three stories, Lucy's original name was the Spanish *Lucia* and the town only became Lucy in 1914, nine years after it had been established by homesteaders; it makes a person wonder who Lucia was.

So the post office opened in 1908 as Lucia, and the village would eventually have two general stores, a one-room schoolhouse, a 16 × 40-foot Santa Fe depot, and a dozen homes. A four-room hotel was built in the fall of 1917. Lucy actually had three schoolhouses over the course of its life, the first being used only until 1910. A second school operated into 1920 and had an average attendance of eighteen

There is no longer anyone waiting back at the ranch in Lucy, NM.

Tumbleweeds accumulate inside the Lucy Ranch.

pupils, all the children found within a radius of 9 miles—at least, all the children that wanted to go to school. The last school was fairly large and was used from 1920 into the 1940s. These schools were the center of the community.

Church was also held in the schools, and often the congregations—Methodist and Baptist—had to lead their own services as the ministers could not make it to town every Sunday. It is said there was a lot of singing in Lucy, and much of the population would head down to the depot to see the passenger train come through from the east once each day. Flour sacks frequently provided the material to clothe Lucy's citizens.

By the 1920s and 1930s, it started to get even more difficult to make a living in Lucy. Families began leaving, and during the Dust Bowl, it became nearly impossible for farmers to tough it out. Often, a homestead would be abandoned in the middle of the night, the residents unable to pay their debts. This was quite a blow to store owners, who had extended credit in many cases and now had to try to absorb the losses. Other homesteaders sold out to ranchers.

As the calendar turned to 1940, there were no longer enough students to justify keeping the Lucy school open and the few children in the area began to be bussed to nearby Willard. The post office closed in 1942. The rail depot was moved to Estancia and later ended up on a local ranch. The last event of real note in Lucy was a train wreck on April 14, 1979, in which forty-two cars derailed, spilling a load of Lincoln Continentals and Ford Broncos all over the tracks.

I got to Lucy in the summer of 2014, just in time to realize I was late. The beautiful skeletal concrete remains of the 1919–1940s school had been razed by a new property owner. Also, the A. D. Formwalt home, at the north end of town, had recently burned. I do not know what caused the blaze, but there was very little left of what looked like a once-charming old farmstead. One of the worst things that can happen to a ghost town hunter is to find that an opportunity to see the past has been lost forever.

Most houses in Lucy were built on a foundation of rock or bare ground, and not a trace of them remains. Luckily, the large, wooden Lucy Ranch is still standing and very photogenic. Also, the Lucy Cemetery has recently undergone an extensive and loving restoration. So there is some activity yet in this little ghost town, one of many forgotten places to be seen along Highway 60.

Captured here is most of what is left of the village of Lucy.

The Williams' homestead in Negra, NM, is eerily peaceful.

44

Paying a Visit to the Williams: Negra

Negra, New Mexico, a few miles east of Lucy, was—like many towns along Highway 60—born when the AT&SF constructed the Belen Cutoff. The Cutoff enabled trains to pass through the flat central plains and avoid climbing into the northern mountains through Raton Pass. The rails came through about 1905, and Negra's post office was established in 1909. However, the post office did not last long; it was shuttered in 1918.

There are a couple stories about how Negra ("black" in Spanish) got its name, including one about a black dog hanging around the early town site. In *The Place Names of New Mexico*, Robert Julyan suggests the town was named for the black soil in the area and mentions the early presence of a water tank colored black. The tank is notable because Negra must have had good water and plenty of it. For instance, Encino, 5 miles east, once got their water from Negra. I was told that a man named Tenorio used a small tanker truck to haul water to town and sell it to residents. Of course, the steam-powered locomotives would have stopped in Negra to get water, as well. After the conversion to diesel engines, the town of Vaughn, another 15 miles beyond Encino, bought four wells in Negra from the railroad for water. At some point, even Duran, 20 miles to the south, got water from the little village.

Near the highway is an empty but nicely intact filling station that might be from as early as the 1920s. Behind it is an old tourist court. Both were built by C. E. Davenport, Negra's first postmaster. A working ranch—the Davenport Ranch—is adjacent to the south. Even farther to the south, across the still-active railroad tracks, is a cemetery. To the west, where most of the community once was, only a few buildings remain. Two of them, not much more than piles of sticks now, were an old school and a teacher's residence.

However, the gem of Negra is a wonderful rock house, built on the site of an old grocery store, and its attendant barn and outbuildings. Despite the general paucity of local historical documentation, in a happy twist of fate, it is known who called this lovely place home. Not long ago, there were four beautiful, southwestern-themed murals on the adobe walls of the high school gymnasium in Encino, now sadly torn down. Those murals were done in the very early 1940s by Hallie Williams; she lived here with her husband, Albert (nicknamed "Ollie"). Hallie also painted at least one other mural and I have been told it still exists, in a store built by Mr. Williams in the 1950s, also in Encino.

Mr. Williams ran a filling station in Negra—likely the vintage one mentioned above. He also operated a mercantile that fronted the railroad tracks in Encino. This store reportedly contained a very smelly stuffed buffalo head on a wall. Later,

Above left: This old adobe awaits its certain fate on the eastern plains.

Above right: The implements of a mid-twentieth century farm life still scatter the Williams' property.

There is plenty vacancy at the Encino Motel on New Mexico's premier ghost town highway.

in the mid-1940s, Mr. Williams built a smaller store on the north side of Highway 60. His third store in Encino, then, would be the one containing the mural. Despite my best efforts, I have never figured out how to see the inside.

Now, there are some abandoned places that feel nothing but creepy and leaving them brings an undeniable sense of relief. Then there are other locations, like Claunch and the Williams' homestead, that are peaceful, if not downright relaxing. With the sun and clouds playing across the endless horizon and a cool breeze rustling the grass, I could have stayed here—and, indeed, in all of what remains of Negra—for many more hours than I did. I hope to return someday. I feel like there is more to be learned out there.

AFTER THE DEPOT: ENCINO

If you drop "Encino" into your internet search engine of choice, most of what you are going to learn is that the population was ninety-four in 2000 and the town encompasses all of 2 square miles. The name Encino, which means "oak" in Spanish, was derived from the scrubby trees that once covered the central plains of New Mexico. As happened often in this dry region, Encino's location can be traced back to the presence of a spring, which had long been a well-known stop for travelers. Prior to 1900, something like a fort was built nearby to accommodate the dusty, thirsty, and weary for an evening or two.

Bonnie Salas was the first to homestead the land that would become Encino, and at that time, the few people in the area were mostly raising sheep or cattle on a fairly large scale. In 1905, the railroad announced plans to establish a depot in Encino and people took notice. This was clearly another common story out on the plains, and one that ended similarly for Encino, as we will see.

The Bond family bought 40 acres from Bonnie Salas, some of which they would soon sell to the AT&SF Railway for the depot. That same year they also built the B. G. Bond Mercantile, which doubled as the depot for a bit and remained the only store in Encino until A. R. Cecil established a lumber company in 1908.

Encino's post office opened earlier, in 1904, and both a Protestant and Catholic church were built, at least one of which doubled as a school. In 1910, the *Encino Progress* newspaper was founded and quickly went out of business. The *Encino Enterprise* gave the newspaper trade another shot in the 1920s and managed to hold on for about a decade. Somewhere in there, Williams' Mercantile was built along Railroad Street and later moved to abut Highway 60.

Above left: The now-collapsed Harrison house was home to thirteen kids and featured a five-seat outhouse.

Above right: The name of two-term New Mexico governor R. C. Dillon can still be seen on the store he once operated.

On the left was Garcia & Sons General Merchandise and on the right the U & I Bar, both owned by Blas and Ursula Garcia. They sold their businesses in the 1970s but lived the rest of their lives in Encino.

The best-known citizen of Encino is undoubtedly R. C. Dillon, elected the eighth governor of New Mexico in 1927. While Governor Dillon was born in St. Louis and moved to Springer, NM, when he was twelve, he later worked at B. G. Bond's Mercantile and eventually opened his own store, R. C. Dillon & Company. The building is still standing and recognizable by its faded sign.

Dillon served two two-year terms and would sometimes have political friends over for dinner at his home in Encino. The governor was also a big proponent of paving roads—not a surprising interest given the muddy, bumpy tracks he would have had to travel. Highway 60 was originally a wagon route, and it was not until 1918 that it began to see some initial truck traffic. Even once cars became relatively popular, horse and buggy was often still the faster way to travel through the area. While U.S. Highway 60 was officially designated in 1926, parts of the route in New Mexico actually remained unpaved into the 1950s.

In 1965, Encino's railroad depot closed, and few small towns could weather that particular blow unscathed. The high school closed in 1982, and many of the town's adobe buildings are now melting back into the earth. Sadly, one building that had to finally be torn down was the old WPA-built gymnasium, which contained the southwestern-themed murals of Hallie Williams, painted for $20 each between 1939 and 1942. On my first trip to Encino, I could have seen them, had I only known they were there. Like so many treasures in life, you really do need to know where to look and when.

CROSS ROAD BLUES: VAUGHN

Several years ago, Vaughn, New Mexico, was probably best known for its police force, which consisted of a single drug-sniffing dog named Nikka. There had been a police chief, but he owed tens of thousands of dollars in child support and was accused of selling one of the town's rifles and keeping the proceeds. A second officer then pleaded guilty to assault and battery, but he was never officially certified anyway. That left Nikka and the Guadalupe County Sheriff's Department to keep the peace in Vaughn, which, despite being considered a stopover for drug smugglers, probably was not totally beyond their abilities. Happily, Vaughn, with a population of almost 450 (down from 539 in 2000), has a couple officers back on the sleepy beat, but it was not always as quiet as it is today.

In 1905, Vaughn was selected to be where the AT&SF and El Paso & Southern Railroads intersected, the only place in New Mexico where two major railways crossed. It was also a division point for the railroad, with a roundhouse, multiple

The echoes from endless nights at Spurs Saloon still ring down Highway 60.

tracks, and a railroad office. After the arrival of the automobile, it became the town where three U.S. Highways—54, 60, and 285—met.

Yet before Vaughn even had a name, it was a favored resting place during drives on the Stinson Cattle Trail. Jim Stinson worked for the New Mexico Land and Livestock Company and, beginning in 1882, would bring up to 20,000 head of cattle at a time from Texas to homesteads and forts in the Estancia Valley of east-central New Mexico.

Vaughn got its name from Major G. W. Vaughn, who was a civil engineer for the AT&SF. Right off the bat, there was a water shortage. In 1908, the AT&SF built a water tank and two underground cisterns to try to collect as much of the precious liquid as they could. Drinking water was brought in by tanker from nearby Willard and Negra. The El Paso & Southern did a little better, having their water transported via wooden pipe from Bonito Lake, 100 miles to the southwest. In 1909, the AT&SF figured it would just be easier to pay the El Paso & Southern 24 cents per thousand gallons than try to collect their own water any longer.

In 1910, the Los Chavez Harvey House opened, named after the Chavez family, who arrived in the area with Juan de Oñate and the first European settlers in the late 1500s. The Harvey House in Vaughn served as kind of a minor league team for newly recruited Harvey Girls, who were just learning the proper way to be cordial. The hotel itself never saw many guests and closed in 1936.

Charles Lindbergh even stopped in Vaughn, but not because he particularly wanted to. In 1928, engine failure forced him to land his plane and wait in town a few days for a replacement part to arrive. He stayed at the Harvey House, and

One of two garages operated by A. R. Allen in Vaughn.

Several murals are hidden inside the ruins of this bar. Painted around the time of the Great Depression, they are signed by "Vagabond Artist," a drifter who reportedly worked in exchange for room, board, and alcohol.

apparently, despite the best efforts of the girls, he was not interested in socializing with them in the slightest.

Vaughn was not incorporated until 1919, but by 1920, it had a relatively healthy population of about 1,000. However, the number of residents may never have climbed much higher than that. One Harvey Girl, Alice Garnas, said in 1926: "Vaughn was a shocking place. There was no place to go, nothing to do. Just Vaughn and those wide plains on all sides—cattle country. But it was for me."

It might be for you, too. Yet if, like many, you are just passing through, try to make a stop at Penny's Diner. Look for the restaurant at the crossroads that appears to be inside a large aluminum Airstream trailer. Once you enter, it will be 1955 all over again, and you may just hear that clickity-clack as the iron horses continue to rumble through all these years down the road.

THE RUINS BY THE RAILS: RICARDO

Ricardo is yet another of the many towns that came to life seemingly overnight as the AT&SF built the Belen Cutoff through the middle part of New Mexico. Located in De Baca County, a few miles south of Highway 60, the recorded history of Ricardo appears to be scant at best. The village's name is thought to have been that of a railroad official, and Ricardo, right along the tracks, operated as an AT&SF section house and water station.

Sadly, on the night of May 6, 1908, a massive fire started in the large Grosh and Strayhorn store, spreading to the Ricardo Hotel, the barbershop, and most of the town. The *Santa Fe New Mexican* said that Ricardo was "reduced to ashes." However, rebuilding commenced, and a post office opened the same year, doing business until 1956, after which the mail went to Fort Sumner. There was also a schoolhouse. In the late-1950s, the school was purchased and hauled away so the lumber could be reused. A vintage photo of the train depot would seem to indicate that Ricardo at one point had "the one and ONLY flower garden" in De Baca County.

While virtually none of Ricardo is as it was (the post office became part of a ranch home; a general store collapsed), one gem does persist—at least for now—and that is a wonderful and spacious two-story adobe structure, which may have been constructed in 1908 as a tuberculosis sanatorium that never held any patients. In the late 1920s, it's said that locomotive firemen who provided assistance shoveling coal to get freight trains up the long hill to Vaughn were briefly stationed here. It was headquarters to the adjacent ranch, as well. A later renovation for a family home was found to be impossible and now it is quite near collapse. However, having

Above left: A stone-lined walkway still leads to the last place in Ricardo, NM.

Above right: The staircase to the second story of the majestic adobe.

become the lone sentinel over this tiny corner of the plains, much of its old charm and majesty remains. It is not hard to imagine a family tending the stone walkway or perhaps lounging on the porch of a fine spring morning, the wildflowers blooming way-off into the distance. Beneath the prairie wind, you can almost hear boots slowly climbing the shattered wooden stairs.

You do not have to listen hard to hear the cows, though, a couple dozen of which may be quite excited to see you until they learn you have no food. Then they just seem vaguely hostile. I should also mention that not only is Ricardo remote, but it is on private ranchland. At one time, I thought it might have been owned by the railroad, but that is not the case. So unless you have an invitation and a way with cows, it is best not to just show up on the porch of the last house in Ricardo.

LIFE (AND DEATH) BY RAILROAD: YESO

Many of the ghost towns I have visited have been written about by Philip Varney in *New Mexico's Best Ghost Towns: A Practical Guide*. The problem is that this book was first published in 1981 and thus many of the photographs and descriptions date from the late 1970s. When I go to check out one of these towns for myself, I usually find much less than he did. Well, what should I expect, as we are talking well over three decades of exposure to elements both natural and man-made? However, Yeso, located along U.S. Highway 60 as one heads toward Texas, is a ghost town that may actually look fairly similar to how it did when Varney stopped by. It should also be pointed out that Yeso is not entirely a ghost town; a few people do live here, and a functioning post office sits right across the street from the abandoned one.

Yeso the settlement sprang up along Yeso Creek, but the water was not entirely fit for consumption. Yeso translates as "gypsum" or "chalk" in Spanish, and you cannot really drink a glass of dissolved gypsum without running into problems. Yet Yeso also had readily accessible groundwater that could be pumped for livestock and locomotive engines traveling the newly built Belen Cutoff, away from the steep grades toward Colorado. One of the first frame train depots was built in Yeso, formally established in 1906, a year before completion of the Cutoff.

The town did alright for a while. A post office was constructed in 1909, and the AT&SF kept things going despite a lingering regional drought. Yeso quickly became a gathering place for the ranchers and handful of farmers in the area. Oddly and inexplicably, the spelling of Yeso was changed to a misspelling ("Yesso") between 1912 and 1913. Then things got rough after World War II, when diesel locomotives were introduced and trains no longer had to stop in town to take on water. That was also about the time it finally became clear that the land around Yeso was really not very good for farming and might not be suited for much beyond grazing sheep. It had been an awfully dry few decades, too.

By the mid-1960s, the school—built by the WPA in 1940—closed as the remaining steam locomotives were retired. The old frame train depot then became one of the last of its kind to fold, shutting its doors for good in 1968. Most everyone packed up and moved to Fort Sumner, 22 miles east. Apparently, four families opted to stay in Yeso and I have to wonder if their descendants occupy the couple of well-maintained homes fronting U.S. 60.

Much remains of Yeso, including the still-decaying ruins of several old houses—an entire abandoned neighborhood, more or less. There is also the Frontier Musem [*sic*.] (once known as the Hotel Mesa), as well as the shell of the Super Service Drive In garage. Yet there have been some casualties. What Varney described as a

Above left: The Hotel Mesa ended its life as the Frontier Musem [*sic.*].

Above right: Despite the vehicles passing by on Highway 60, it has been a long time since the Super Service Drive-In saw any customers.

Water was the reason for Yeso's settlement, but the amount and quality has never been assured.

possible gas station, garage, motel, and residence complex on the east end of town has largely collapsed, although you can still find the date of construction—June 8, 1929—set in the cement out front in bottle caps if you look carefully. Several other structures are also showing their years. So if you are going to visit, I still would not recommend waiting very long.

WHISKEY AND THE DEVIL: TAIBAN

If you travel Highway 60 farther east through New Mexico, past Yeso and Fort Sumner (the likeliest final resting place of Billy the Kid), you will come to the unincorporated town of Taiban. Taiban is known for its old Presbyterian Church—a lonely, gutted house of worship visited by photographers and the traveling faithful. The church, once part of a neighborhood that included homes, businesses, and the two-story Taiban High School, now sits off by itself on the prairie. Not a single privately-owned business remains in Taiban—just the post office persists—but it was not always this way.

Like Yeso, Taiban was named for a nearby creek. The source of Taiban Creek was Taiban Spring, originally known as Brazil Spring after a Portugese immigrant. Manuel Brazil, who arrived in 1871, was the first recorded settler in the area. The meaning of the word "Taiban" is obscure, although it is thought it might be a Navajo or Comanche word for "horsetail," a reference either to a local plant or to three small tributaries that flowed into the creek. It is said that Billy the Kid watered his horse at Taiban Spring.

Also like Yeso, Taiban was founded in 1906, when the tracks of the Belen Cutoff came through, redirecting rail traffic from the mountainous north. A school was built, and contracts were drawn for the construction of fifty homes. By 1907, there was a bank and a hotel. In 1908, the AT&SF began actively encouraging settlement of the region. Over 1,600 emigrant trains passed through the plains that year, bringing homesteaders from Oklahoma, Kansas, Missouri, Texas, and beyond. However, the vast majority did not settle in Taiban, and in 1909, the town's population peaked at 400 residents. These were mostly farmers and sheepherders, already veterans of conflict with both the landscape and established ranching interests.

In the fall of 1908, construction began on the First Presbyterian Church of Taiban. It was completed on December 22 at a cost of $250. Less than $100 of that could be covered by the congregation, necessitating loans from the ladies of the Baptist Church and the Taiban Savings Bank. The first sermon, given by Reverend John R. Gass, was sparsely attended due to cold weather.

The First Presbyterian Church of Taiban, NM, stands iconic on the plains.

Above left: The Taiban Trading Post has been closed for many years now.

Above right: Colorful wallpaper in this collapsed kitchen is a reminder of more hopeful times.

Shortly after Taiban was founded, a heated controversy erupted over the construction of the Pink Pony Saloon and Dance Hall, which, in addition to selling alcohol, was to later hold cockfights and house a snake den in its basement. Opened a bit east of the church and amid great consternation, the Pink Pony became the only one of forty private businesses operating in Taiban in 1908 to survive into the latter part of the 1930s.

One settler, Vane Outias, described his experience arriving in Taiban:

> There we were. Piling down off the steps of the jerk-water train at Taiban, New Mexico; Pa, Ma, and the kids. After counting the suitcases, the packages, and the bundles, Ma called the roll. All were present. The bunch of us with Ma herding started for the hotel. We had come out here to file on some land: make a living farming; and when we had proved-up, sell out and go back east (rich).
>
> On the way to the hotel I made observations for my own particular benefit, namely, there were two places in town which would have thrown Carrie Nation into a frenzy if she had been one of our party. Watch me hurry, as I had come from a dry state. Just as soon as I could find an excuse I was admitted to the bar of the first emporium. I meant to say; when I found an excuse that the Missus would accept.

Thus alcohol and religion squared off, vying for the soul of Taiban, whose heart was being broken by the farming of an inhospitable and increasingly barren land. Some years, the church won out and Taiban was proclaimed dry. Other years, liquor laws were overturned, and Taiban was once again wet. As the Depression and drought deepened, families left the area. Following Prohibition, it was largely the availability of liquor that kept the place from blowing away entirely. For nearly all of the town's existence, the Presbyterian church had played a vital role in the spiritual life of the community, also serving Methodists and Baptists. Yet with congregations dwindling, the last service was held in 1936.

After World War II, only seven businesses operated in Taiban and the population fell to fifty. The bars were the most successful, and customers from dry counties in Texas and Oklahoma came out for a drink. The town even had an airfield—Taiban International Airport—and the wealthy would fly themselves in to purchase booze. People as far away as Western Oklahoma knew of Taiban's reputation as the "boot-legging capital" of Eastern New Mexico and West Texas.

Yet alcohol is not enough to save a town that has lost all hope of real prosperity. Passenger and express train service ceased in 1933, the same year telegraph service ended. New highways and decades of difficult-to-impossible dry farming steadily drove nearly all the residents of Taiban elsewhere. By 1960, only one business remained besides the post office—Mac's Bar. Now that is gone, too, having burned in the mid-1980s.

This unique home in Taiban includes chicken wire construction and an alcove in the gable.

While the battle between God and alcohol played out for many years in Taiban, walking its streets reveals no clear winner. The bars are all turned to dust and the little church stands vacant and exposed; its bell tower was removed in 1960, the baby grand piano is long-sold, and the doors and windows have been destroyed by vandals. So I guess we could call it a draw, for now. On the other hand, visitors sometimes write prayers on the walls of the alcove of the church, behind where the old walnut pulpit used to stand. Perhaps the little wooden building, now over 110 years old and my favorite place to photograph in the entire state, has life yet.

4

THE EASTERN PLAINS

Dominated by farm and ranchland, a portion of this area lays atop the massive Llano Estacado, or "Staked Plain," a legendary tableland that has been the backdrop for much happiness and hardship.

LITTLE PLACE ON THE PRAIRIE: DUNLAP

The Homestead Act of 1862 was an attempt by the U.S. government to entice citizens to open up the West by offering 160 surveyed acres in exchange for a five-year commitment to reside on the property. Untold numbers of people who could not afford their own farms and ranches or struggled at difficult factory jobs in crowded cities thought that sounded pretty good, and they quickly hitched up their wagons or hopped on a train.

This sometimes isolated and remote land was often agreed to sight-unseen by would-be homesteaders and, while many did find fields fertile for farming, others did not. Some then tried to eke out a living as best they could; others got right back on the next train heading in the direction from which they had just come. While the history of Dunlap, New Mexico, does not go back quite as far as 1862, the homesteading spirit was evident in those who settled this sparsely populated part of the eastern plains.

It was W. O. Dunlap who founded this outpost in De Baca County, about 35 miles southwest of Fort Sumner, and gave it its name. He scouted parcels for incoming homesteaders and a community developed. In 1907, a post office opened. However, as the years passed, many in Dunlap began to find it harder and harder to survive off this land, and most eventually left—most, that is, but not all. In fact, Dunlap persists as a small, close-knit rural community to this day.

Above left: For decades this little building was the heart of Dunlap, NM.

Above right: Now even the ruins of the Dunlap Community Church and School have collapsed in a ruin.

The post office closed in 1961, possibly taking the general store with it. No evidence of either remains. Yet, really, the heart of the area beat in the lone building they once stood next to—the Dunlap Community Church and School. Worship, academic instruction, important discussions, and just plain-old get-togethers all happened in this little place on the prairie. Sadly, since these photos were taken, it has largely collapsed.

There is not much documentation of Dunlap that I can find, and perhaps the best look back has come from people who shared their memories on the City of Dust Facebook page:

Our ranch was the closest to the school. Once one of the teachers lived in our bunkhouse. Miss McCoy, I believe. My mother played the piano for all the plays and programs! No one's mentioned the dances! Hot times Dunlap!

My family and our friends share a long memory of a uniquely close life in an isolated area, but the memories of those times do not fade at all in my heart.—S. SoRelle

My family homesteaded and ranched in this area, and my grandmother, her brother, and my dad all attended school here. Dunlap was the hub of the ranching community. Dances and other social events were held in that building. It was a school, church, and community gathering place. There was also a post office and general store there.

My grandmother used to ride her horse—or drive a horse and buggy—to the school. My dad, his cousins, and several friends all attended school there until they completed 8th grade, when they transferred to different high schools. My dad's last year there was around 1955. I last attended a church service there in the early 1980's, right before I left for college.—JDW

The Dunlap Church and School in its final days upright.

Thanks very much to SS and JDW for providing the kind of remembrances you cannot find through Google. Finally, I will note that the land on which the ruins of the Dunlap Church and School rest is privately owned. You know what that means.

A Tale of Two Towns: Acme and Frazier

Those of you who are fans of the Roadrunner and Wile E. Coyote might be excited to hear that there was once a town in New Mexico named Acme. However, the corporation that lent its name to the place made cement blocks, not jet-propelled unicycles. In the early 1900s, the Acme Gypsum Cement Company built a mill slightly south of the Clovis Highway (supplanted by present-day U.S. 70), 17 miles northeast of Roswell, where aliens would later badly botch a saucer landing.

In 1907, the Acme School commenced lessons from inside a tent. Later, a one-room frame-and-plaster school was built on the western edge of town, placed so as to keep the students away from the dust and smoke of the mill. Grades one to eight were taught there, and kids had to bring their own books and supplies, along with their lunches.

Acme boasted a hotel, a large horse barn, a general store, a depot, and some company houses for workers. Its post office opened in 1906 and closed in 1946, by which time the Acme Gypsum Cement Co. had been out of business for ten years. When the mill closed, it was estimated that there were between thirty and

Above left: The last one-teacher school built in Chaves County now serves a population of zero.

Above right: The elegant remains of the stone Frazier School.

forty people in Acme, of which twenty were children. Now there is nothing left of Acme at all, except for the cemetery, north of U.S. 70, half a mile from where the mill once crunched gypsum.

About 300 feet from what does not remain of Acme is the photogenic ruin of the Frazier School. So close together that some people do not really distinguish between Acme and Frazier, their existence overlapped slightly. Frazier was established later and survived longer, but not too much longer. Frazier's post office and school opened in 1937, a year after the Acme mill closed. Funeral services were held in the school since the Acme Cemetery was nearby. I assume that anyone who died in Frazier was also buried in the Acme Cemetery. I also assume funerals were not held during class, unless mortuary science was on the curriculum.

This was a community of folks trying to make it through the Great Depression as best they could. Many of those who worked at the Acme Gypsum Cement Co. had moved on and about the only employment in the area was found in the dusty, meagre soil of the eastern plains. There were some cattle, and one enterprising rancher is said to have herded turkeys as if they were sheep. Coyote skins could be sold at Bond-Baker Wool and Hide Co. for $1.50–$5 per pelt, and the meat of a cottontail rabbit might be worth $1. Many families lived in dugouts or other similarly challenging shelter.

Yet these homesteaders wanted their children to receive a good education. So C. M. Martin, the Chaves County superintendent, designated that a new school, larger than the one in Acme, be built on land donated by Otis L. Shields. Then Lake J. Frazier secured a contract with the WPA for construction, and thus both the school

A view of the combination cistern and coal storage tower as once seen by students.

and the community were named for him. This would be the last one-teacher school built in Chaves County.

Stones were gathered from the area for building material, and black volcanic rocks framed the windows and doors. White rocks were used to create a five-point star above the front entrance, and a steer's head with longhorns was set in the eastern wall. There was one double-size room with a smaller room on each side partitioned by double doors. There was no electricity, but six large north-facing windows let in plenty of sunlight, nor was there running water—just a stone tower out back with a cistern on top, as well as coal storage below. "WATER" was spelled-out in the volcanic rock along the tower's top. Mesquite roots augmented the coal supply when it came to providing heat, and teachers were required to check the route for rattlesnakes before allowing a child to use the outhouse.

As soon as it was completed, pupils attending the Acme School moved to the Frazier School, as did their teacher, Margaret Harrison. There were twenty-four kids that first year, and Mrs. Harrison boarded with the family of Mac Smith, who ran a store and gas station, as well as the post office. Some students walked to school, but those on ranches were picked up in a car. Horse-drawn implements were used to make the roads suitable for busses. Mrs. Harrison had already moved to another school by 1938 and later teachers came and went frequently in Frazier.

Frazier was an active community through World War II, but at the end of the war, enrollment in the school dropped below the mandatory eight pupils and it closed in 1945. Students in the area were then sent to Roswell. For a time, the school was used as a community center, however, even the need for that finally withered. Now, not a soul remains in Frazier and the ruins of the stone school, once the pride of many, are all that marks this place.

IN THE SHADOW OF THE BUFFALO HUNTERS: CAUSEY

Causey, New Mexico, is located in Roosevelt County at the crossroads of NM 114 and 321, 35 miles southeast of Portales and about a mile from Texas. Despite some previous conjecture that the moniker was intended to flatter a railroad vice president and get a line through Causey, it now seems agreed upon that the town was named for at least two of the Causey brothers—T. L. "George" and John. The brothers were buffalo hunters, working in the southeastern part of the state and George, in particular, established a reputation for being one of the most successful in the history of the American West. Estimates by outside observers put the number of buffalo he killed at around 40,000. One of George's hunting companions, George Jefferson, known as "Old Jeff," said "Causey killed more buffaloes in one winter … than Buffalo Bill Cody killed in his entire lifetime."

The problem with shooting that many buffalo is that eventually you run out. Of course, that is how it went, and after hunting through the 1870s, by 1882, Causey and his comrades had shot the last of the wild buffalo on what is known as the Llano Estacado ("Staked Plain") of Eastern New Mexico.

While George Causey generally operated to the south, the town of Causey is on the west central part of the Llano Estacado, one of the largest tablelands in North America, the majority of which is in Northwest Texas. The explorer Coronado had this to say upon stumbling onto the Llano in 1541:

> I reached some plains so vast, that I did not find their limit anywhere I went, although I traveled over them for more than 300 leagues...with no more land marks than if we had been swallowed up by the sea...there was not a stone, nor bit of rising ground, nor a tree, nor a shrub, nor anything to go by.

To translate for those of us no longer using leagues, Coronado covered more than 1,000 miles.

Turning his attention from buffalo hunting to cattle ranching on the Llano, George Causey established a ranch south of Lovington, about 60 miles from present-day Causey. Mr. Causey promoted the suitability of Eastern New Mexico for livestock and farming, and as one of the earliest settlers in the area, he opened it up for those who followed, not least by being the first to discover the rich supply of groundwater in the region.

In 1902, Causey was thrown from a horse during a mustang round-up, badly injuring his spine. After traveling all over the country depleting his finances in a failed effort to find medical relief for his severe headaches, and increasingly disenchanted with the rapidly changing West, Causey sold his ranch to pay off

Above left: A dairy barn in Causey, NM, is reclaimed by nature.

Above right: This massive gym is now home to the metallic bones of an array of heavy equipment.

debt, married his nurse, and moved near Kenna, 30 miles southwest of the town that bears his family name. He shot himself in his bed on May 19, 1903, his body discovered by his nephews, Vivian and Ralph, who had heard the report of their uncle's gun.

I do not know if Causey had been established by the time George Causey died. The earliest date I can put on the name is 1907, when the post office opened. It remains operational to this day. The town site was actually moved by Ezra Ball sometime after World War I and is now 3 miles north of where it was first established. These days, you will find some well-kept homes and a few residents there. The population as of the 2000 census was fifty-two, and it has probably decreased a little. There is also the ruin of a massive WPA-built school, which is collapsing into the overgrowth. It seems surprising that such a large school existed in Causey, but F. Stanley reported in *The Causey (New Mexico) Story*, published in 1966, that there were over 150 students attending the school in 1942. Here is a taste of how things were back then:

> The Causey school has over fifty in high school and over one hundred in grade school, Supt. L. E. O'Hare stated last weekend. The attendance has been good. The school board has not decided when it will dismiss school for crop gathering, but Supt. O'Hare is of the opinion it will be about the first of next month. There have been no resignations of teachers so far. (Sept. 7, 1942)

Beverly Wood once lived in Causey.

Also, in 1960, the senior class was said to have visited the "Insane Asylum" in Las Vegas, NM, as part of a long field trip. I wonder if the kids lobbied to put that on the itinerary.

Stanley himself said of Causey, "The most surprising thing is the school system and the fire house, worthy of larger cities." He went on:

> Time is unimportant to the teachers. They give so much of it to the school. Many a trip took me through Causey and teachers would be noted at their desks far into the night. There may be a thousand reasons for this; there may be none save that they love their work.

Next to the school is a massive metal armory-like structure with a caved-in roof—one of two gyms. This bigger one was probably built in the mid-to-late 1960s. However, it may not have been used as such for long because the school closed sometime in 1970 or 1971. Stanley noted that, "Causey had a long, hard road to travel, but it has made the grade and the future looks good." It is referred to as "one of the business centers of Roosevelt County," with a population of 234 as early as 1920. Like so many small rural towns, the future Stanley spoke of appears to have, in the end, been at least as hard as the past.

A LITTLE PIECE OF QUIET: LINGO

The little village of Lingo, which, as of recently, could still claim at least one family as residents, is on the eastern edge of New Mexico, just 5 miles from Texas. It is a tiny dot on the map at the western extremity of the staggeringly vast Llano Estacado plateau.

Jean M. Burrough's *Roosevelt County History and Heritage* leads off with a hand-written letter about the Bilberry family's arrival in what was not yet Lingo. They lived in a "two-room shack, dirt floor," and Finis Bilberry farmed and raised sheep. School was first held in 1916, the schoolhouse being a one-room dug-out at a place then regrettably named Nigger Hill. Also known as Dead Negro Hill, this was where, in July 1877, a group of African-American soldiers and buffalo hunters abandoned their pursuit of some Comanche who had stolen stock and killed one hunter. Desperate and dying of thirst in the summer heat, the men began to search for water, some going eighty-six hours without a drink. Five would die in this incident, which was sometimes remembered as the "Staked Plains Horror." Finally, in 2005, the name of the rise was officially changed to Buffalo Soldier Hill.

Speaking of place names, in *The Place Names of New Mexico*, Robert Julyan notes that Lingo was known as Need in 1916, becoming Lingo in 1918. No one knows why it was originally called Need, but in 1918, the postal authorities thought the name too close to Weed, a settlement down south in Otero County. At that point, not only did Need become Lingo, but the post office got moved 3 miles to the north. I do not know why the post office also had to move. Anyway, it has been speculated that Lingo took its name from the way the people spoke (i.e. "the jargon, slang, or argot, of a particular field, group, or individual"), but more probably it references a family, now forgotten.

I have often felt that City of Dust is in a race against dusty oblivion as so many of the buildings I have documented are disappearing fast, and those in Lingo are no different. Here, unlike in Lucy, I arrived just in the nick of time to photograph the post office, where around 1953, a Mrs. Balko was postmistress. Mrs. Fanny Brown took the position on April 20, 1968, staying until the post office closed in 1984. I visited on December 12, 2015, and on the following Valentine's Day, the old post office burned to the ground. Apparently, someone was driving a pick-up with a BBQ grill in the back and hot coals became airborne. Numerous blazes were started, consuming a total of 1,083 acres in southeastern Roosevelt County, but at least no one was hurt and no other structures were damaged.

Also found in Lingo is the crumbling Baptist church, reportedly once used by other denominations on occasion, possibly after a second church in town

Above left: Lingo's general store fronts quiet Highway 114.

Above right: Of a variety of former commercial concerns in Lingo, none remain open.

Above left: Lingo's old post office burned to the ground mere months after this shot was taken.

Above right: A storm gathers over the ruins of the Baptist church.

closed. The general store is still standing, as well. Other buildings once included a café, hardware store, basketball gym, and a shop in a Quonset hut, none of which exist today.

Fish fries and dances were held at the high school, which was across the street from the post office. The dances were a big deal as such frivolity was not allowed in nearby Causey. However, Causey was where you would go to get your hair styled by the much-loved Lingo resident Edna Ashbrook. Lingo's last graduating class was in 1945 and numbered five: Meryl Terry, Pete Rogers, Billy Joe Cunningham, Otis Foster, and Gene Collins. You can still find the blacksmith shop, but it has fallen into a jumbled heap. Things are certainly much quieter than when Lingo could boast of the Hair twins (Judson and Jettie) and the Henry triplets (Anna, Bunna, and Lanna), although, you know, quiet can be nice.

A LIVELY AND ENERGETIC PLACE: PEP

The first thing that strikes one about Pep, at least before visiting, is its name. It might seem a little unusual, even more so because there is another town called Pep 60 miles dead east in Texas. In fact, it has been said that Pep, New Mexico, got its name directly from Pep, Texas. It has also been said that Pep was named for a fortified breakfast cereal popular during the Depression. Neither of those stories is true though, and in reality, Pep was probably named for the reason you would guess at first glance.

The place that became Pep was settled in the fall of 1925 by Edward Cox, who established the first residence and store. T. M. Pearce, in *New Mexico Place Names*, concluded that Pep got its name because Cox expected it to be a "lively and energetic place." Apparently "pep" was a word used often during the Depression to instill enthusiasm. That is how Texas got its Pep, too.

I have been told that there was a big party to get the town going, including a baseball game and rodeo. The post office opened in 1936—possibly beating Pep, TX, to the name—and remains in operation to this day, despite there being only a handful of residents left. The post office also serves the ranches and farms of the surrounding area, but it is now only open in the morning and mail is not delivered every day.

Pep is in Roosevelt County, on the western edge of the legendary rangeland known as the Llano Estacado, or "Staked Plain." I described the 37,000-sq. mile Llano Estacado a bit when we explored nearby Causey. There is a lot of folklore surrounding why this formidable mesa is known as the Staked Plain. The term is

Edward Cox, the founder of Pep, NM, hoped that it would live up to its name.

Life on the plains of Pep was never guaranteed.

perhaps better translated as "Palisaded Plain," the "palisaded" likely referring to the high, rocky escarpments that border the tableland, particularly to the east, where one—the Caprock Escarpment—reaches 300 feet tall. A common, but probably less accurate, explanation is that the "stakes" are really the dried shoots of yuccas, which can rise a few feet above ground and thus appear as scattered stakes when one looks out over the landscape. My favorite is that early settlers "staked" their trails with buffalo bones and skulls so that they could follow them back out if they got lost, like macabre breadcrumbs. Recently, it has been said that "*estacado*" may actually be incorrect and that the original Spanish word could've been "*estancada*" or "ponded." Indeed, after a rainfall, water collects in the small depressions across the landscape and thus "Ponded Plain" might be fitting. As for which is right, I would do like everyone else does and just go with whatever you like best.

As for local personages, author Jack Williamson was from Pep and taught at nearby Eastern New Mexico University in Portales. Known as the "Dean of Science Fiction," he published in every decade from the 1920s to the 2000s. He also built a little wooden cabin near his parent's house in the 1930s so he could write undistracted. There is even a small tub—more of a shallow metal box, really—inside so that he could bathe and continue writing with minimal interruption. Fans make pilgrimages to the cabin, but Mr. Williamson did not want the structure maintained or moved after his death in 2006 at age ninety-eight.

So why did Pep not live up to its name? Initially, Cox, who owned all the land in town, may have tried to sell it at too high a price during a bad economic time for the country. Maybe it was the name in the first place; Pep, TX, has wound up in a similar state. Yet the record on Pep is spare, to say the least.

While it is difficult to uncover the history of the little town, let alone the stories of the people that lived there, that does not make Pep unimportant. In fact, I would argue, quite the opposite. When I posted a photo from Pep on the City of Dust Facebook page, a comment was made that says more in a few words than I probably have in this whole piece:

This post may be the only place in the entire world where the old community of Pep is being discussed. Pause for a moment, if you will, to honor those who gave their all here—gambling on a new life—in the Great American Desert.—G. Lucas.

Famous science fiction author Jack Williamson began his writing career in this handmade shack.

There is a lot of room on the Staked Plain, as long as you don't want hills.

ON THE EDGE OF THE STAKED PLAIN: HOUSE

The Llano Estacado, or "Staked Plain," the massive tableland covering 37,000 square miles of West Texas and Eastern New Mexico, is fascinating and evocative. We have visited Causey and Pep, both on the western terminus of the Llano, so let us visit another Llano town. This one is right beside the Mescalero Escarpment, a long cliff averaging about 200 feet high and forming the Staked Plain's western edge. The Mescalero Escarpment could be (and probably was) seen as an excellent defense against enemies below. House, New Mexico, sits 15 miles northeast of where this escarpment descends from Taiban Mesa into the wonderful semi-ghost town of Taiban.

Near House is another simply named town called Field, and while the origin of Field's name is obscure, it would seem kind of obvious to anyone passing through. Likewise, you might think that perhaps House was named for a house. In fact, it was named for John L. House and his family, who settled on the current town site in 1902. John built the first store in 1904, and within two years, House had a post office, with Lucie Jordan House as the first postmistress. I have heard that settlers often arrived by train from Tucumcari and made the surely difficult journey up the escarpment to House on foot, where an agent would assign them land to homestead.

Below the soil of much of the Llano Estacado is caliche, a hard mineral here known as "caprock." In fact, the entire top of the plateau is often referred to as "The Caprock," or even just "The Cap." To make things more confusing, the towering escarpment on the Texas side is the Caprock Escarpment. Anyway, this Caprock caliche can keep soil depth relatively shallow, and without any features to block the wind, the Llano region was one of the two most devastated by the Dust Bowl, particularly in Texas. Southeastern Colorado to Southwestern Kansas was the other hard-hit area. I wonder how House fared.

There are no descendants of the House family in the area any longer, but the town that bears their name persists, and House is not a ghost by any stretch. While the 2000 census puts the population at seventy-two, House feels somewhat larger. There are many well-maintained homes and gardens, and it comes across as an active place. I humbly apologize to the residents of House for making their home look a little like a real ghost town; I guess it is just what I do.

While not a ghost town, House has nevertheless changed considerably over the decades. Its history is difficult to uncover, but someone whose family settled near House in 1906 and who began attending school there in 1948 told me that the town once had four service stations, three churches, three grocery stores, three mechanic shops, two hardware stores, two feed stores, an appliance store, a barber shop, a blacksmith shop, a cafe, a school, a pool hall, a movie theater, a post office, and a potato grading shed. Besides the post office and school, virtually none of it remains.

Above left: House, NM, is on the edge of the Llano Estacado, one of North America's largest mesas.

Above right: This long-shuttered commercial building is located in the midst of 37,000 sq. miles of very flat land.

The Sunshine Grocery has been eclipsed.

In 1948, 325 kids attended first to twelfth grades in House, and almost every quarter section was occupied by a family. Just a handful of years later, there were 125 students. Much of this decline occurred in the 1950s, when New Mexico suffered another terrible drought and people left the farms around House *en masse*.

That is a bit of history about the town itself. However, I would be remiss in not mentioning Glen Franklin, born in House on March 18, 1936. Mr. Franklin was world tie-down roping champion in 1965, 1967, and 1968, and inducted into the ProRodeo Hall of Fame in 1979. It is said that Mr. Franklin carried a rope while still in diapers and was soon looping every dog, chicken, or human that crossed his path. He rode a horse named "Red Light" that received its share of credit for Mr. Franklin's achievements. As time passed, Mr. Franklin did not want to travel constantly, and he retired from rodeoing to ranch near House, which he was still doing well into the 2010s.

GET THE MOTOR RUNNING: HIGHWAY

Let us make some concessions to time with a snack-sized piece on the tiny dot on the map of Eastern New Mexico known as Highway, our last stop out here. Located on NM Highway 206 between Pep and Milnesand, perhaps 12 miles from the Texas line, Highway got its name because it is located on a state highway. Locals will tell you it should be "Hiway," but the NM Department of Transportation has other ideas. There is not a post office, and I do not think there ever was one, although there are a few inhabitants.

The building pictured below is probably the most prominent in Highway (or Hiway) and was a welding and mechanic shop for many years. At first, the construction had me thinking it might have been a church or school. Oscar "Pouch" Lott lived and worked here most of his life and still maintains the reputation of having been the best blacksmith in the area.

Highway is in Roosevelt County, on the extreme western edge of that mighty chunk of flat earth known as the Llano Estacado. Much has already been said about that legendary landscape in the previous sections on the nearby towns of Causey, Pep, and House.

Blink and you will miss Highway, NM.

I think this structure had something to do with water.

5

ROUTE 66

From 1926–1937, travelers headed west on Route 66 in New Mexico went north just beyond Santa Rosa, up through Santa Fe, and then south past Albuquerque all the way to Los Lunas. After 1937, the road was straightened, cutting off these north-south jags and traveling directly east-west through Albuquerque. Interstate 40, which traces a significant portion of Route 66 through the state, was the Mother Road's true death knell.

WHERE THE CROWS FLEW: CUERVO

When it comes to ghost towns, it can be the best of times and the worst of times in Cuervo, New Mexico. Its condition is remarkable not just because the town is no secret, as any internet search will attest, but because it is literally feet from Interstate 40. Clearly, most people on the road between Albuquerque and Tucumcari do not stop for a visit. Either they do not know about Cuervo or they do not care, which is fine with me, although it certainly does not keep all the riff-raff out.

Pulling into desolate, (mostly) deserted Cuervo is like driving into the apocalypse, if the apocalypse happened in 1920. Just forget about the semis whizzing by, and there are only old cars and older houses, piles of clothes, and newspapers from decades ago, everything in that hauntingly arrested state that all aficionados of the lost desire.

It is always useful to understand the names of places, regardless of the language they are in, and that is true in Cuervo. The town's name means "crow" (or, alternatively, "raven"), and while there may once have been many of these dark birds around, I have never seen one in Cuervo. Perhaps they hang out on nearby Cuervo Hill, the town's namesake, or, maybe, unlike me, they are simply smart enough to stay out of the relentless heat of the midday sun.

A renovation has forever altered this timeless scene in the red stone school of Cuervo, NM.

Cuervo's residents came to this building to mail letters and buy groceries.

Like so many others in New Mexico, Cuervo was a railroad town, brought to life about 1902 when the Chicago, Rock Island, and Pacific Railroad came through and turned the little outpost into a water stop. Before that, the town site had been on a trade route in use since at least the early 1500s. Yet no Europeans had previously thought to try to settle down way out on the wide and lonely plains.

Cuervo continued to grow as a wave of increased cattle and sheep ranching swept through the area in 1910. Sixteen years later, Route 66 ran straight through town, easily supporting the few gas stations and commercial enterprises that sprang up in its wake. At its height, Cuervo had two of everything a person could want: schools, churches, doctors, and hotels.

One school, built around 1930 and closed in 1958, stands alone in a field of red dirt and was the high point of my first visit to Cuervo. It was later bought and turned into what appears to be a home but may not be for all I know. Also, both churches are still standing. The Catholic church on the south side of I-40 was built of red sandstone during World War I. It is well-maintained, holding services to this day. The Getty Baptist Church also made of red stone, on the north side of the interstate, was once a barn. It is not well-maintained to this day.

As with dozens of towns that owed their existence to the railroad and Route 66, the construction of the interstate system was a harbinger of doom. In the case of Cuervo, in the late 1960s, I-40 followed the Mother Road right through the center of town, probably turning the lives of many residents into something like a John Mellencamp song.

Yet it is worth bearing in mind that Cuervo was never a metropolis. Its population in 1946, immediately post-World War II, was only 128. In 1981, Philip Varney reported in *New Mexico's Best Ghost Towns: A Practical Guide* that many homes remained occupied. Now its population may be in the single digits, including the owner of the semi-functioning gas station on the north side of I-40. If you came to take pictures, I hear he will not be happy to see you. He may well have good reason as Cuervo has a reputation for being alarmingly creepy, and many people have told me they have left quickly after being followed by slow-moving vehicles. I have had some unpleasant times there myself. So, despite Cuervo's obvious allure, I am going to end this piece by not being the one to encourage you to visit.

The cryptic interior of a former home in Cuervo.

Many of Cuervo's homes are still standing, each with its own character.

Getting Less Kicks: Newkirk

Newkirk, New Mexico, is a bit of an enigma. It does not show up in ghost town books—perhaps because a handful of people still live there—but this old stopover on Route 66 consists mostly of abandoned gas stations and stores from the days when the Mother Road kept a steady flow of paying customers coming through. In fact, the only going concern in Newkirk now, as far as I can tell, is the Phillips 66 station where old Route 66 meets the I-40 ramp.

Founded in 1901 with the construction of the nearby railroad, Newkirk was originally known as Conant, the name of a rancher in the area. This was later changed to Newkirk, in honor of a town in Oklahoma from which a resident hailed. Route 66 began to bring people to Newkirk in the 1930s, when the population reached 240 residents. Yet, by the 1940s, despite having four gas stations, two restaurants, De Baca's Trading Post, a post office, and some rental cabins for travelers, the population was back down to 115.

Wilkerson's Store survived for many years after the decimation of Route 66 by Interstate 40 in the 1960s. Of course, interstate bypasses, such as those that cut-off Newkirk and nearby Cuervo, led to the collapse of the economies of many small towns that depended on travelers. The store was open until 1989, when the Wilkerson family finally had to walk away. It was a Gulf Station, though you could not tell that now. Collapsing adobe is slowly bringing the building back to earth.

Reportedly not open nearly as long but now holding up better is the old post office, gas station, and store. Built in 1910 with large stones, it must have been fairly bustling for decades, which is quite hard to imagine now. It still retains a good bit of its dignity though and is my favorite building in Newkirk.

I have seen references to an old bar and restaurant called Carlo's Place and an ancient Shamrock Gas Station, but either they have fallen down or I have overlooked them. There are also the remains of a store that sold "figural bottles." Apparently, these were bottles made into the shapes of figures.

These days, Newkirk seems to have largely returned to its ranching roots. Yet perhaps things are not as pastoral as they seem. A photographer I know was once standing right on the side of old Route 66 with her camera when a State Trooper raced up and told her she was "in danger." "People around here shoot first and ask questions later," he said, before speeding away again.

My visit was much less dramatic and included a stop at the Phillips 66 to buy an iced tea, ask a question of the owner, and pet his massive German shepherd. However, after the State Police dubbed I-40 a "River of Crime" in 2013, estimating that an astounding one in seven vehicles were potentially involved in criminal activity, perhaps the residents of Newkirk were right to be on edge. If you are planning to visit, it is best to be prudent.

Above left: There is only one place for gas in Newkirk, NM, and it is not here.

Above right: Wilkerson's Store, once a Gulf Station, was open until 1989.

Built in 1910, well before Route 66, this stone post office and gas station is a testament to sturdy construction.

ALMOST NO KICKS: MONTOYA

If you drive east from Newkirk on old Route 66, at some point, you will cross what was once the Goodnight-Loving Trail, one of the most famous cattle drives of the American West. In the mid-1860s, thousands of cattle and somewhat fewer cowboys began to travel this route from central Texas to Fort Sumner, New Mexico, not 50 miles south of Newkirk. Soon, the trail was extended to Denver and then Cheyenne, Wyoming.

The Goodnight-Loving Trail would encompass one of the West's great stories when, in 1867, Oliver Loving, the trail's namesake alongside Charles Goodnight, was undertaking an ill-advised daytime ride during a cattle drive from Texas to Fort Sumner, straight through Comanche country. He was accompanied by a young colleague named "One-Armed" Bill Wilson. The two were indeed attacked, not far from Carlsbad; Loving was shot, and after lying near the Pecos River for a couple of days while Wilson heroically went back to alert Goodnight, would develop gangrene in his arm. Loving crawled back to the trail and was finally taken to Fort Sumner by Mexican traders, but allegedly the local surgeon hesitated to amputate as he had never removed a limb. Goodnight arrived and insisted that the arm be taken off, but it was too late and Loving died shortly afterward. This tale is largely retold in Larry McMurtry's famous—if fictionalized—*Lonesome Dove*.

You will not see as many cattle now, but you will want to keep your eyes open for Montoya because if you blink, you might miss it. There is just not much left. Originally a sparsely populated village known as Roundtree, Montoya's story begins the way of so many towns that are now ghosts. That is, it was summoned to life by the power of the railroad. Thus, Montoya was officially founded in 1902, when it became a center for shipping and freight on the Southern Pacific.

Richardson's Store and Sinclair Station is one of a couple ruins that remain in Montoya. Richardson's opened in 1925, the year before Route 66 was established, and would have served countless travelers. Maybe my uncle made a stop on his trip from the Midwest to California back in the '50s. The store survived into the mid-1970s, when it was finally locked up with all the unsold merchandise inside. After the owner died in the early 1990s, Charles B. Dominguez, a family friend, was asked to watch over the place and its still-unsold contents for a few weeks. Dominguez ended up minding the store for at least ten years, never selling a thing. What has happened since then, I cannot say, but Richardson's Store has finally collapsed.

There is also a two-story house made of rock constructed by Sylvan R. Hendren and Maria Ignacia Ulibarri Hendren in the early 1900s. Containing a kitchen and living room on the lower level and two bedrooms upstairs, it was known as Casa Alta ("High House"). It has a distinctive sloping roof used to catch rain for a cistern,

Above: Somebody opened fire on this ruined bar in Montoya, NM.

Below: Richardson's Store opened in 1925, a year before Route 66 arrived. It has now collapsed.

but you will have to take someone else's word for it because I did not actually see it. Like I said, blink and you will miss it.

Route 66 from Montoya to Tucumcari, the next town to the east, is narrow and often flooded after rain. In fact, I had to get out and throw rocks into the water at the lowest points of the road to make sure we would not be partially submerged in a large sedan. A narrow, one-lane tunnel eventually takes you to the south side of I-40 and, as you hope that any oncoming traffic—however unlikely—is paying attention, it is hard not to wonder if Route 66 was always this difficult and dangerous. Of course, it was much more so.

6

SOUTHWESTERN NEW MEXICO

Beyond the larger towns of Silver City and Truth or Consequences are a constellation of historic ghost, semi-ghost, and downright alive towns, most of them originally settled near mining operations. This region of New Mexico was known the world over for its silver deposits, but gold, copper, zinc, and more could all be found in the ground, both then and now.

A Resurrection: Chloride

I will admit that many of the places I visit can appear run-down and lonesome and the tales may get a little dark. Sure, I guess I like it that way. Yet this piece will be a little ray of sunshine—do not worry; it will not last long.

Chloride, New Mexico (pop. about ten), has risen like a phoenix from the ashes to become a true ghost town no longer, but a fascinating Old West museum piece. It is like stepping into a land that time literally forgot, but it has not always been this way.

First of all, Chloride is a bit out of the way. You have to follow Highway 52 west, way out, past Winston (founded by citizens who thought Chloride was too rowdy to abide), and then turn onto a gravel road amusingly named Wall Street. When Wall Street ends smack dab up against the Gila National Forest, you will know you are there. I have absolutely no idea how folks managed to get to the place before there were roads. Yet, in 1879, Harry Pye, an Englishman, was somehow hauling a wagon load of supplies north to Ojo Caliente for the army. As the sun began to set, he decided to seek shelter from the Apaches that populated the area. When he awoke, he saw silver chloride nearby and later came back with some friends to stake a claim. Again, if you see the landscape surrounding Chloride, you cannot help but wonder about the agony that must have been inherent in the simple statement "came back." I do not know how Mr. Pye even found the claim again.

Both the Pioneer Store and Monte Cristo Saloon have been given new life in Chloride, NM.

Once an early saloon, this building was the post office until it closed for good in 1956–7.

In any case, the tent city that sprang up was called Pyetown and then Bromide and finally Chloride for that first silver chloride find. Within a couple of years, hundreds of miners had flocked to the area to seek their fortunes near the "Pye Lode." However, by this time, Pye himself was already dead, having been killed by Apaches regardless of his best efforts shortly after his return. Despite being somewhat dark, I suppose it is just the nature of the time and place. Pye was eulogized as being "an honest, sober, and industrious young man and a good miner and prospector. He had many friends in camp." However, people always say very nice things about you when you are dead.

In Pye's absence, Chloride boomed a bit and was soon the center for all silver mining in the surrounding area. However, the young town was apparently 100 percent male, and it has been reported that free property was offered to the first woman brave (or foolish) enough to set up housekeeping. Property (or perhaps a seat on the town council) was also to be given to the father of the first baby, "If it is known who he is." I wonder if that got the ladies flocking to Chloride. I also wonder if it is true.

Something that definitely is not true is the accepted size of Chloride's boom. Most sources state that Chloride peaked in the 1880s with a population of up to 3,000. In order of likely importance, there were eight (or nine) saloons, an assay office, three general stores, a stage line, restaurants, butcher shops, a candy store, a lawyer's office, a doctor's office, a hotel, boarding houses, and a Chinese laundry. However, contemporary sources, such as the 1884 edition of the N. W. Ayer & Sons *American Newspaper Annual*, put the population at 200 or even below. You can surely reduce the attendant infrastructure proportionally. Yet eventually, some ladies must have arrived, and at least one brothel opened. Being so remote, the railroad never made it out, which was somewhat unusual for a relatively active mining town. Transportation was only via stages and wagons.

Regardless of its true size, by the turn of the century, the price of silver was dropping and so were hopes for Chloride's future. When Philip Varney visited in the 1970s to do a feature for his book *New Mexico's Best Ghost Towns: A Practical Guide*, the town was as one might dream a ghost town would be: historic, desolate, and beautifully intact. Varney says as much in the introduction to his piece.

Looking at Varney's pictures, it is hard not to want to have seen Chloride in its virtually abandoned state. The photo of Chloride's two major false front buildings— one a general store, the other the old Monte Cristo Saloon—from Varney's visit is particularly appealing. Yet perhaps that is strengthened because we now know what had been collecting dust and dirt and bat guano inside the building with the faded "Pioneer Store" signage when that black and white shot was taken.

Above left: A sample of the fashions for offer in the early 1920s.

Above right: Tools, housewares, and more were waiting in the Pioneer Store, now all lovingly cleaned and displayed.

The Pioneer Store was built in 1880 by James Dalglish, who had come from Canada hoping that the high desert would help his ailing health. He ran the store through 1897 and sold absolutely anything anyone could want in a town like Chloride. As mining waned, the store was sold and then sold again with a family named James finally running the place until nearly every resident of Chloride had moved away. That was in about 1923. At that point, the store was closed with all the merchandise sealed-up inside, which was how it stayed for several decades.

In the late 1980s, Mr. and Mrs. Edmund moved to Chloride and met a Mr. James. He agreed to sell the store to the couple, and in 1989, they began the massive job of cleaning up the place and its contents, which included items spanning its entire history from 1880–1923. We are talking such things as partly full whiskey bottles, farm implements, clothes, kitchen wares, and Native American artifacts. The clean-up process was not completed until 1998, but now, the Pioneer Store is a museum showcasing much of what it sold in its heyday. It is pretty incredible, and a person has to see it for themselves to truly appreciate how rare and fascinating a find this is.

Mrs. Edmund was very generous with her time during our visit, telling us about individual items and the painstaking process of bringing everything back to life. Then she took us next door to the Monte Cristo Saloon, now an art gallery and store.

I bought some artisan honey from (relatively) nearby Hillsboro because I really like honey. A walking tour led us past the old "hangin' tree" and another old saloon that became the post office until it, too, closed. Only one person was ever hanged from the "hangin' tree" (and he by effigy), but numerous drunks were reportedly chained to it until they sobered up. There is an odd building called the "Doodle Dum," built by its owner in 1920 out of stone and with a steeply pitched roof to withstand the fierce hailstorm that he believed God was preparing for mankind. Original law offices and the U.S. Treasury Mining Company Headquarters also still stand.

All-in-all, I have never seen a ghost town brought back to life so effectively while maintaining its sense of remoteness, both in time and place. It is utterly charming. You have really got to go to Chloride sometime.

THIS IS NOT A GHOST TOWN: HILLSBORO

Hillsboro, 20 miles west of I-25 on NM 152 (aka the scenic route to Silver City), at the foot of the Black Range Mountains, is not a ghost town, as anyone that lives there will tell you. Yet it is also not quite the place it was in the early 1890s, when just over 1,500 people called it home. Perhaps one-third of these residents were children—evidence of something like family values, which was a bit unusual in a Wild West mining town of the time. As of the 2010 census, Hillsboro's population was 124.

Hillsboro was certainly a mining town, and a gold mining one at that. In April 1877, Dan Dugan and Dave Stitzel found color along Percha Creek, just beside present-day Hillsboro; suddenly, a rush was on. Four months after Dugan and Stitzel had their ore assayed at $160 worth of gold to the ton, someone built a house nearby; by December, with fresh claims springing up all around, it was decided to christen the newborn town.

I put a lot of effort into describing the origins of the names of places, but Hillsboro seems easy—everyone says they pulled the name out of a hat. Originally, it was Hillsborough, but all those extra letters were quickly deemed unnecessary. Yet a lesser-known version has it that Joseph Trimbel Yankie, possibly the third prospector to arrive in the area, was given the honor of choosing the name. As he was from Hillsboro, Ohio, he chose to the same name: Hillsboro. This account is now considered correct; when in doubt, always pick the less-interesting story.

Within two years, Hillsboro had a population of 300, as well as saloons, grocery stores, and a post office. It also had a problem with Apache attacks, so four companies of soldiers were stationed nearby to provide protection. Once, when Victorio, warrior and chief of the Warm Springs band, went raiding, everyone moved across the mountains to the now-vanished mining camp of Georgetown to wait things out.

The Hillsboro Courthouse saw some notorious cases.

Hillsboro's jail, built in the mid-1890s, once housed rancher Oliver Lee.

A lot of money was soon being pulled out of the region and Hillbsoro became a center of activity, as well as the Sierra County seat in 1884, resulting in the construction of an ornate, two-story brick courthouse for $17,000 in 1892. The sturdy, red-brick Union Church was also built that year. In the end, $6 million in gold and silver was found in the rugged landscape, with all the attendant trading, banking, ranching, and rabble-rousing such a thing would engender. Stagecoaches ran back and forth between Black Range towns and, of course, they were often robbed, so the jail was plenty big.

Hillsboro's last jail, a stone affair built near the courthouse in the mid-1890s, housed some interesting people, including Oliver Lee, James Gilliland, and William McNew, the three accused in the infamous 1896 disappearance near White Sands of Judge Albert J. Fountain and his eight-year-old son, Henry. Fountain had been indicting suspected cattle thieves in Lincoln, and Lee, Gilliland, and McNew had each been named. Incidentally, despite having been an outspoken opponent of Billy the Kid and his gang, Fountain had been selected to defend Billy in his 1881 trial for the murder of Sheriff William Brady, a case he obviously lost.

In 1899, after Lee and Gilliland had escaped Sheriff Pat Garrett, and following political wrangling too labyrinthine to go into here, the accused were brought to Hillsboro, the trial having been moved from Las Cruces at the defense's request. Oliver Lee and Jim Gilliland were tried for the murder of Henry but not his father, and despite blood and signs of struggle at the scene of the alleged crime, there were still no bodies to prove that anyone was actually dead. Lee and Gilliland were found "not guilty" after deliberations that may (or may not) have taken less than eight minutes. Descriptions of the trial scene were wildly embellished; charges against McNew were dismissed. The case has never been solved.

Valentina Madrid, a sixteen-year-old girl, and her seventeen-year-old friend, Alma Lyons, also knew the jail. In 1907, they were accused of poisoning Valentina's husband by sprinkling his coffee with "Rough on Rats" for a week. The girls said they were forced to do it by Valetina's would-be suitor, Francisco Baca, though he was acquitted. The girls were sentenced to be hanged, but public outcry got them life sentences. Thirteen years later, both girls were pardoned by Governor Octaviano Larrazolo on the condition they secure "honorable employment," remain in New Mexico, and never set foot in Sierra County again.

Hillsboro had already begun a steep decline by the late 1890s but revived a bit during World War I. It started to slide again in the 1930s, although after a devastating flood in June 1914, the town was never really going to be the same anyway. In 1938, Hillsboro lost the county seat to Hot Springs (now Truth or Consequences). The story goes that residents of Hillsboro kept traveling to Hot Springs to bring all

Hillsboro, NM, remains a functioning community, as Our Lady of Guadalupe Catholic Church attests.

the county's files and documents back to Hillsboro. This allegedly happened so often that the courthouse was finally taken apart brick by brick, so there would no longer be anywhere in Hillsboro to return the files to. Whether that is true or if the courthouse in Hillsboro was simply sold in 1939 for $440 to provide construction material for the new one in Hot Springs, I cannot say. The courthouse may even have remained whole into the mid-1940s, but it was never entirely dismantled and what remains is a picturesque ruin.

Evidence of Hillsboro's past is all around, including in the Black Range Museum, once the Ocean Grove Hotel. The hotel also functioned as a high-end brothel established in 1886 by a twenty-one-year-old named Sarah Jane Creech, better known as Madame Sadie Orchard, and usually (and mistakenly) said to be British. Among other things, Sadie and her girls are storied for fearlessly tending to the town's residents during the influenza pandemic of 1918. Careful though—corroborating primary source material is elusive.

Hillsboro's present is as a charming small town nestled in the Black Range with a couple cafes and restaurants and the Enchanted Villa Bed and Breakfast, built in 1941. While there might not be much gold in them thar hills anymore, there is still plenty of reason to stay in Hillsboro.

THE WAY THINGS WERE NOT: KINGSTON

Like Hillsboro, Kingston, New Mexico, is not exactly a ghost town, but it is also not the place where "you couldn't walk ninety feet in 30 minutes for the crowd," as it reportedly was on nights after local miners were paid—a place with twenty-two saloons, fourteen grocery stores, three hotels, three concurrently operating newspapers, an opera house, and a school; a place where the bank once held $7,000,000 in silver and the population topped 7,000. It is not that place now, and it never was that place. There may be few Old West mining boom towns that have had their history so exaggerated. It has even been said that Kingston was once the biggest town in territorial New Mexico.

Everyone agrees that in the early 1880s, precious metals, particularly silver, were found in the area. Ralph Looney's *Haunted Highways* says that Kingston's establishment can be traced to a drunkard, Jack Sheddon, who became such a nuisance in nearby Lake Valley that the sheriff put him on a burro with food and whiskey and sent him north. *En route* to Chloride, he made a stop near what would become Kingston, had a good long drink, and passed out on a rock. When he came to, he noticed that his stony pillow had flecks of metal in it. This was bornite (a silver ore), and he quickly established the Solitaire Mine. Soon, prospectors were descending from every direction. It is a great tale, but not true. Prospecting was underway before Sheddon even arrived (he did at least exist) as a few miners had already moved the 10 or so miles west from Hillsboro, which had been established in 1877.

In the fall of 1882, James Porter Parker, General George A. Custer's former roommate at West Point, platted Kingston, which took its name from a local mine—the Iron King. Soon it was reported by the Tombstone Epitaph in Arizona that there were forty-five men working area mines. By 1885, a year after Kingston's oft-reported peak population of 7,000, Territorial Census figures show 329 residents in Kingston and the adjacent Danville Camp combined, even with Spanish and Chinese included in the tally.

It may well have been a rowdy place though. In an 1886 edition of the *St. John's Herald* out of east-central Arizona (at the time, Kingston did not even have one newspaper), a citizen expressed upset at their town's lack of a school, church, or, indeed, any public institution. Reverend S. W. Thornton even referred to Kingston as "the typical mining town in all its wickedness." In 1888, construction of a stone church began, which would serve Kingston's now 1,000 residents. Sometimes claimed to have been spontaneously financed by prostitutes, gamblers, and dance hall girls, it is more likely that a Reverend N. W. Chase and local Methodists solicited the funds.

Above left: A long road of misinformation leads to the Kingston, NM, of the late 1800s.

Above right: Unusual things still happen in Kingston.

In 1890, according to the U.S. Census Bureau, Kingston's population reached 1,449, a count it probably never surpassed by much. The 1893 economic panic sent silver prices crashing and the number of Kingston's occupants plummeting back into the low hundreds at best. By the time it was really all over in the early 1900s, almost $7,000,000 in precious metal had indeed been mined in the vicinity, not an inconsiderable sum. Yet it had taken over twenty years; that amount was never in the Percha Bank at one time.

Even the usually no-nonsense Philip Varney slips up when it comes to Kingston, mentioning in *New Mexico's Best Ghost Towns: A Practical Guide* that Chief Victorio's band of Apaches once descended on the town. However, because the miners were assembling a hunting party and had their firearms at hand, they quickly drove the attackers out. It is said Victorio decided to leave Kingston alone after that and the happy populace named their new three-story hotel "The Victorio" in the chief's honor. The problem is that Victorio died in 1880, two years before Kingston was established. It is not really Varney's fault; there are many tales about Victorio and his band's depredations in and around Kingston, and Varney did not have Wikipedia in the late 1970s.

You may also hear of the ironically named Virtue Street, site of an infamous Kingston brothel. While you will find a very short side street named Virtue today, it was probably created after Kingston's initial abandonment, but do not fret—the world has not gone entirely topsy-turvy; there certainly was a brothel in early Kingston.

Walking the two short thoroughfares, many have surely wondered how a town could rise and fall so precipitously. Since it did not, it is not as surprising that only one historic building exists wholly intact: the Percha Bank. The old assay office, remodeled as a private home, and a vastly reconfigured hotel—The Victorio—also persist. Floods and fires have certainly done their damage, but there was never so much to disappear as is usually imagined.

Much of the confusion over Kingston is attributable to James A. McKenna's classic *Black Range Tales*, which it should be noted contains the word "tales" in the title, not "facts." Some of McKenna's yarns, which many ghost town sources reference, take place in a Kingston of 7,000 rabble-rousers. This "the metropolis of the Southwest," while possibly true to the spirit of the day, never quite existed. In 1936, the same year that *Black Range Tales* was published, Madame Sadie Orchard (a.k.a. Sarah Jane Creech) told an interviewer of a peak population of 5,000. Few having actually been there, such wild exaggerations made their way into the Kingston literature. In the end, maybe the Kingston of myth is just one of those places in the Wild West of our collective imagination that people wanted to exist so badly that it has been wished into being. It is not the worst thing to have happened to history, I suppose.

The Percha Bank is the only historic building that is as it used to be in Kingston.

THE BRIDAL CHAMBER: LAKE VALLEY

Lake Valley lies in the shadow of Monument Peak (a.k.a. "Lizard Mountain"), a prominent knob of rock that nevertheless would have given early travelers no indication of the great wealth hidden nearby. It was 1878 when Union Army soldier George W. Lufkin and his partner, Chris Watson, went looking for silver not far from Hillsboro. A Chinese man had told Lufkin and Watson in a Georgetown, New Mexico, saloon of how he had ended up lost on the way to Silver City and come across a piece of silver chloride, or "horn silver," a pure, soft form of the mineral. Yet he could never find where it came from again. That would certainly be a likely story in the Old West. However, Lufkin and Watson were in their mid-fifties and desperate for a strike, and they thought what they had heard had the ring of truth. Thus, they went out looking for silver on a search that lasted weeks—with no luck, naturally. Then the story gets contentious, but everyone agrees that somehow Lufkin and Watson stumbled upon silver outcrops. Unfortunately, they had now been out so long that their initial grubstake was exhausted and they had to quickly head back to Hillsboro to raise more money.

After an additional delay due to Apache depredations, the two miners eventually got back to work, hauling out a half ton of ore and bringing it directly to the Red Onion Saloon in Silver City. Here, John A. Miller saw what had been found and offered the men $1.50 a pound or $1,500 for the whole load. Miller went to the assay office, where the geology was better than in the saloon, and quickly learned that the ore ran $12 per pound. So he put up enough money for him, Lufkin, and Watson to mine in earnest.

In the spring of 1881, the men sold their claim to a syndicate led by a man named George Daly. Miller got $100,000 while Lufkin and Watson, along with nine other men, each got $25,000, in addition to the considerable amount they had already made. Lufkin would build a house nearby in a camp he named after Daly, but the settlement soon moved and became known as Lake Valley in honor of a small lake nearby, long since gone dry.

Then John Leavitt, a blacksmith, leased a claim from the Sierra Grande Mining Company (in which Walt Whitman owned 200 shares) and spent two days digging in a hole that Lufkin and Watson had started. Lufkin and Watson should have gone farther though because at 10 feet, Leavitt hit a thing that most miners surely did not even dare dream of—a cave of solid silver chloride measuring 26 feet wide and 12 feet high. A flame could melt silver right off the ceiling. Despite all this, Leavitt did not seem to know what he had discovered and sold his claim back to the Sierra Grande Mining Company for a few thousand dollars.

The Bridal Chamber Mine produced 2.5 million ounces of silver in Lake Valley, NM.

The Lake Valley School is now a wonderful museum devoted to the ghost town and surrounding area.

Of a dirty gray color and very malleable, horn silver was soon being cut into large blocks and loaded into railroad cars parked right outside the cave. The ore was so rich it did not even need to be smelted. A massive piece valued at $7,000 (about 394 pounds worth, silver then being $1.11 an ounce) was exhibited at the Denver Exposition of 1882. No single concentration of silver has ever exceeded what was quickly named the Bridal Chamber for obvious reasons. All told 2.5 million ounces were exhumed in a couple years. This was not even half of the silver taken from the immediate area between 1881 and 1893, when the price of silver collapsed with the end of mandated government purchases. For a few years in the early 1880s, though, Lake Valley was something else.

It is often said that Lake Valley's population peaked at 1,000 in 1884, but the 1885 Territorial Census counted only 183 residents. The town moved once and then again to be closer to the Bridal Chamber. One western surveyor tagged Lake Valley as "the toughest town I've ever seen." He added, "I'm satisfied a man died with his boots on every night." Marshal Jim McIntire was brought into Lake Valley in 1882 to keep the peace at the astounding rate of $300 per month. Those 200 or so folks must have been rowdy indeed. Legendary lawman and strong-arm Jim Courtright was also there and quickly killed two ore thieves in a gunfight. He would kill three more men in Lake Valley.

A number of Lake Valley's souls rest above the ghost town in which they once lived.

Yet if Lake Valley was not lacking for silver or bloodshed, it was not lacking in irony, either. George Daly, who had purchased all those area mining claims initially, was killed by Apaches on the day the Bridal Chamber was unearthed by John Leavitt. About the time Leavitt was digging, an area rancher returned home to find his cabin burned and his wife, Sally, as well as one of his children, missing. He immediately rode to Lake Valley to get help. Sally was found, beaten, but safe, and with her child. Still, things were heated between settlers and the Warm Springs raiders led by Nana, Geronimo's brother-in-law, then in his eighties and still avenging the death of Victorio.

So, that night, a retaliatory ambush was planned. A posse headed to Cotton's Saloon for some liquid courage and to await the arrival of the Buffalo Soldiers of the Army's Ninth Cavalry. Lieutenant George Washington Smith was reluctant to join the attack, but he finally relented and his men accompanied the posse. Nana's camp was found 10 miles west, in Gavilan Canyon, and there, the group charged right into an ambush themselves, with Daly and Lieutenant Smith killed in the initial moments.

As for George Lufkin, who, with Chris Watson, first rediscovered the lost silver near Lake Valley, he was buried in the town's cemetery; he died without a penny to his name and rests in a pauper's grave.

Lake Valley burned in 1895 and was already on its way to becoming a ghost town when a man named Oliver Wilson came to make a home in 1908. He had built the Victorio Hotel in Kingston and refused to sell, only to have the bank eventually foreclose on him. His daughter, Blanche, was nineteen, and as they approached the town, they saw no way that she could remain in Lake Valley. In the end, she stayed until her death on March 31, 1983, running the Continental Oil distributorship for the area, fully taking the reins after her husband, A. Lee Nowlin's death in 1937. Blanche said her family disapproved of her marriage because Lee was from Texas and "Texans generally weren't held in very good repute around here in the old days." Blanche's next-door neighbors in the old Bella Hotel, Pedro and Savina Martinez, were the final holdouts, keeping watch over the town until 1994. Pedro had arrived in Lake Valley in 1904 at the age of two and spent ninety years there.

So why would anyone live nearly alone in a ghost town? Blanche Nowlin said, "It's so peaceful, you know. It's wonderful to wake up in the middle of the night and hear the silence. This is where all my memories are," she continued. "There are seven graves over there on that hillside that I can't leave." Now, she rests among them herself.

The home of Blanche Nowlin until her death on March 31, 1983.

TALL PINES: PINOS ALTOS

About 7 miles north of Silver City, New Mexico, on NM Highway 15, at the gateway to the massive Gila Wilderness Area (created in 1924 by Aldo Leopold as the first designated wilderness in the world) is the small mountain town of Pinos Altos ("Tall Pines"). Sometimes called a ghost town, it is not quite that, although it does owe its existence to that activity common to many true ghost towns: mining. In the case of Pinos Altos, gold was the metal that brought the place to life.

In 1860, Thomas "Three-fingered" Birch, who had been looking for gold for years with no success, got a drink of water from Bear Creek and happened to see the very thing to which he had—until then—fruitlessly devoted his life. The encampment that sprang up around his find—Birchville—bore his name and was perched atop the Continental Divide at just over 7,000 feet. Later that year, Captain Thomas Mastin, after discovering gold-bearing quartz in the area, established the Pacific Mine. Thomas sold the mine to his brother, Virgil, and a short time later, Captain Thomas and three other miners were killed by a group of 400 Apache warriors led by Mangas Colorados ("Red Sleeves") and Chief Cochise, Mangas Colorados' son-in-law. Seven years later, Virgil Mastin would meet a similar fate.

Mangas Colorados is said to have lured other Birchville miners to their deaths by having Indian maidens brush out their hair and perform a bit of strip tease at the top of a hill. When the miners clamored up the hill to get a better look, the Apaches

It never hurts to hang a little luck on your door, even in lovely Pinos Altos, NM.

Built in 1969, the Pinos Altos Opera House was constructed using original material salvaged from vintage buildings.

ambushed them, perhaps killing more than forty. It should be noted that earlier Mangas Colorados had been "invited" to the settlement, only to be tied to a tree and lashed with bullwhips. Thus, as was Chiricahua Apache custom, vengeance upon the miners was uppermost on Mangas Colorados' mind for some time.

During the Civil War, Birchville's population plummeted, mostly because there weren't many able-bodied men left to guard against Apaches. It was occupied by the Confederacy from fall 1861 until shortly after the Union prevailed at the Battle of Glorieta Pass, which took place outside Santa Fe in the spring of 1862. Following the Civil War, Fort Bayard was built to try to protect miners from continued Apache attacks.

Upon resettlement at the war's conclusion, residents seemingly reverted to an older name used by Mexican miners, Pino Alto, which became Pinos Altos. It may also be that Birchville only referred to the mining camp itself, not the entirety of the land that Pinos Altos encompassed. The two names might even have co-existed. In any case, the town of Pinos Altos received a post office in 1866 and became fully legitimate, featuring a saloon, general store, and dueling ground (now the site of St. Alexis Catholic Church). Yet Apache depredations continued to plague the area until 1874, when a deal was struck whereby as long as a cross remained standing on an adjacent mountain, there would be no fighting. Both sides held to the deal, and the cross was upgraded a total of three times, just to be on the safe side. Virtually all the tall ponderosa pines for which the town got its name were cut down by the time of the mining boom years of the late nineteenth century.

Gold and silver mining booms were to come and go in southwestern New Mexico, but the region around Pinos Altos also contained copper, lead, and zinc, so the town continued to prosper. It was not until the 1920s that mining began to wind down for good, at which point over $8 million dollars' worth of minerals had been removed from the surrounding mountains.

Today, Pinos Altos is home to a few hundred people and is a pleasant place to spend some time soaking up all that Wild West history. If you go, you will certainly want to stop by the historic Buckhorn Saloon. Also, check to see if the Pinos Altos Post Office and Ice Cream Parlor is perhaps open for business again. You never know, and the charming building sits on the site of the Norton Store, built around 1890. That store was itself on the site of the Occidental Hotel, a two-story log structure long vanished into the mists of time, like so very much else.

The Gold Avenue Methodist Episcopal Church in Pinos Altos was dedicated in May 1898.

The Buckhorn Saloon (*c.* 1860) dates to the earliest days of Pinos Altos.

For Sale: Fort Bayard

Located 10 miles east of Silver City, Fort Bayard was established in 1866, a direct result of the discovery of gold in nearby Birchville in 1860. As gold brought miners and prospectors to what is now the Gila Wilderness, the Warm Springs Apache did the best they could to drive the new arrivals either back to where they came from or into their graves, whichever came first. So a fort was built and named after Brigadier General George D. Bayard, a frontier fighter with the First Pennsylvania Cavalry who died in the Civil War at Fredericksburg, Virginia.

Initially, Fort Bayard was comprised of some huts made out of logs and adobe—not exactly a formidable defense. Yet by the time serious campaigns were launched against the Chiricahua Apache leaders Victorio and Geronimo, it had grown considerably. The Army often sent African-Americans, so-called Buffalo Soldiers, to battle Native Americans in the West, and such was the case with Fort Bayard.

A monument to one Buffalo Soldier, Corporal Clinton Greaves of Company "C," 9th U.S. Cavalry, stands in the center of the fort. In addition to a statue of a rifleman in action, which may or may not be Corporal Greaves, there is a plaque that reads:

> On June 27, 1877 while on patrol in the Florida Mountains near Deming, New Mexico Corporal Greaves performed an act of heroism saving six soldiers and three Navajo scouts from attack by forty to fifty Chiricahua Apache. Corporal Greaves was awarded the Congressional Medal of Honor on June 26, 1879.

However, in 1886, following the capture of Geronimo, the Apache threat subsided. The 400-acre post remained active until 1900, when Fort Bayard became an army sanatorium and research center for tuberculosis, the climate of the area being quite salutary for TB sufferers. The hospital was briefly transferred to civilian control before a new one, the first built under the auspices of the Veterans Bureau, was constructed in 1922. Here, in a modern facility with a 1,250-patient capacity, victims of mustard and chlorine gas attacks in World War I used mirrors to reflect the plentiful desert sunshine "into" their lungs in the hope it would heal them. During World War II, the fort also housed German prisoners of war. The hospital closed in 2010, following a Department of Justice report citing "life-threatening" conditions, and completion of the nearby (but off-property) Fort Bayard Medical Center.

To me, the most striking part of Fort Bayard, which is both a National Historic Landmark and National Historic District, is Officer's Row (sometimes called Doctor's Row), a shady avenue comprised of several derelict officers' residences that, aside from one that is a museum, resemble abandoned mansions. They

Above left: Many decades after the U.S. military departed Fort Bayard still searches for its purpose.

Above right: Presumably a reasonable likeness of Corporal Clinton Greaves, who received the Congressional Medal of Honor in 1879.

The military families are long gone while Fort Bayard waits patiently for new life.

were built in the 1920s to replace the shoddy original quarters. Numerous smaller homes for enlisted men can also be seen, as well as a historic theater and various intriguing outbuildings.

The 145,000-sq. foot hospital reportedly cost about $100,000 annually to maintain, despite being empty, and was demolished in 2016, just shy of its 100th birthday. Beyond that, the state of New Mexico, which has owned the property since 1965, can hardly afford to tear anything else down, let alone fix it up. Even the trees have been dying from lack of caretaking. So, Fort Bayard was put on the market in 2014. In fact, part of the reason the hospital was demolished was because it was thought the removal of the asbestos-filled building would make the fort more attractive to a future buyer who would then (hopefully) preserve the other structures. So far, there have been no takers.

There have been many worthy ideas for repurposing Fort Bayard, with its lovely old buildings and beautiful, open grounds. Suggestions have ranged from a treatment facility for veterans with post-traumatic stress disorder to a workforce development center to a mixed housing development. Other ideas have included turning the fort into a shelter for homeless vets, opening a private military academy, or creating a ghost-hunting destination. The latter might be one way to meet Corporal Greaves and his companions.

Despite the difficulties, The Fort Bayard Historic Preservation Society, along with the nearby village of Santa Clara, hope the state might finally hand the fort over to them before wholesale demolition is necessary. The preservation society offers excellent guided tours, providing a bit of access and plenty of history, and more can be learned at the Santa Clara-Fort Bayard Visitors Center down the road. Unfortunately, although many people love the place, Fort Bayard proves that the Beatles were incorrect in at least this instance—it is not only love the old fort needs, but money, and quick.

Iron Town: Fierro

A few miles east of Pinos Altos as the crow flies lie what remains of Fierro, New Mexico. For a true ghost town, it has still got a good number of buildings that, while certainly falling, are not completely down and out yet, and it has plenty of lonely charm. All you are likely to hear while exploring is the occasional sound of wood scraping tin when the breeze picks up and maybe the caw of one or two of those massive crows flying overhead.

Fierro is an archaic form of *hierro*, the Spanish word for "iron," and iron is the reason the village was settled in the first place. The mining history goes back to 1841,

You will not find anyone
waiting at home in Fierro, NM.

when Sofio Henkle (or Henkel or Hinkle), a German immigrant living in Mexico, went looking for copper deposits. He found both copper and iron on a mountain a few miles north of the big copper mine in Santa Rita and named the mountain and its new mine Hanover, after his former home. The town just a couple miles south of Fierro would also be called Hanover.

Henkle, however, was soon driven out by hostile Apaches and lucky to escape with his life; he had been warned of an imminent attack by a friendly Apache woman. Henkle returned years later after New Mexico became a U.S. Territory, believing that he would be safe now that the army was guarding the mines. However, the Civil War required most federal soldiers to head east and Apaches and Confederates started raiding. So Henkle gave up for good and lived the rest of his life in the Mesilla Valley far to the southeast.

By the early 1880s, with the threat of Apache raids largely gone and the railroad already having arrived at Silver City—about 15 miles southwest—the Colorado Fuel and Iron Company (CF&I) took an interest in the iron ore deposits of Fierro. A post office was established in 1899, about when the railroad finally reached the village, and as much as ten carloads of ore were being shipped out each day to Pueblo, Colorado, where CF&I was based.

The population of Fierro was 750 in 1920 and probably never reached much over 1,000, even during the peak years between World War I and the start of the Great Depression, by which point 6 million tons of iron had come from Fierro's mines. Some 78 percent of Fierro's population was of Mexican descent in 1920, and that percentage increased, reaching the high nineties once the mines closed.

The mines shut down in 1931, although the large Continental Mine ran intermittently, and tragically, four miners were killed near it in a "short fuse" accident in 1947.

Manuel Araujo's Grocery also housed the post office. It sits on the site of the Phoenix Mercantile (a.k.a. *La Tienda del Finicas*).

While the Cobre Mining Company resumed operations, now with an emphasis on copper, and some residents stayed at least into the 1990s, Fierro never recovered from the economic blows of the early 1930s, when people began to leave quickly, many for gold mines in California.

The Gilchrist and Dawson Store, Mrs. Rel's Rooming House, Filiberto's Variety Store, McCoy's Store and post office, John Oglesby's silent movie house, and Sheriff Mac Minter's pool room were frequented by the miners and their families. Now they are all gone. Some of them burned in a fire in 1923 when a miner from Mogollon went to sleep at Mrs. Rel's following a fandango next door and kicked over a kerosene lamp in his room. Without a fire department, and with some buildings even having sidewalks made of wood, much of Fierro's early commercial district burned quickly. The Phoenix Mercantile (a.k.a. *La Tienda del Finicas* (The Finica's Store)), which even sold fine furniture, would also burn. Manuel Araujo then constructed a grocery store on the site of the mercantile and Araujo's Grocery sold clothes and housed the post office, as well. Sitting on the steps waiting for the mail was a common pastime in Fierro. This rare building still stands, and Mr. Araujo is well-remembered for his generosity to those who couldn't always afford to purchase his wares.

Another building of interest is the little jail by the railroad tracks, near the arroyo that runs through the village. In *Black Range Tales*, James McKenna recalled visiting Fierro in the 1880s and noted that mining towns punished wrongdoers by tying them to a thick log that had been sunk in the earth with 8 feet remaining above ground. Normally prisoners would be released once they had sobered up and calmed down; that could easily take all night. Fierro reportedly did away with its log in the early years, but the sturdy concrete jail probably never held any true desperadoes.

Fierro must not have had many criminals if this cement jail was sufficient.

St. Anthony's Mission Catholic Church in Fierro, built in 1916, still holds services.

Fierro was known for its love of baseball, with three different fields used during its history. In the late 1930s, the team went by the seemingly unusual name "Peru Miners." Basketball was also popular, with games played on the school's dirt court until it was paved in the 1930s. Fierro even had a Boy Scout troop as late as the 1940s.

One interesting tradition in Fierro was *El dia de las Travesuras*, "The Day of Pranks," which was a replacement for Halloween. On that night, there was no trick-or-treating in Fierro. Instead, kids played pranks, the most common of which was to tip over outhouses. One man spent a night in his outhouse with a shotgun to prevent any hijinks, only to have his bathroom toppled anyway when he went back to his house at 2 a.m. for a quick cup of coffee. This never happened to the managers of CF&I as they had indoor plumbing and even electricity. Later, it is said that a popular prank was swapping around railroad and highway signs, which might cause problems regardless of income bracket.

While Fierro is a ghost town now, two places that are very much alive are St. Anthony's Mission Catholic Church, built in 1916 and later enlarged, and, ironically enough, the cemetery, which covers four acres and is lovingly maintained. In addition to bi-weekly services, a celebration and mass are still held at the church every year on June 13, the Feast of St. Anthony. On this day, many of those for whom Fierro remains important meet to reminisce and once again walk the quiet streets of the old village.

Zinc Town: Hanover

Just 3 miles southeast of Fierro is Hanover, New Mexico. Hanover was named by local prospectors for the Hanover Mines near Fierro, which were, in turn, named for Hanover, Germany. Hanover was the hometown of Sofio Henkle, who is credited with discovering iron and copper in the area in 1841 but was forced out by Apaches two years later.

Hanover, however, was not known for copper or iron, but zinc. The post office opened in 1892 and operates to this day, although it has moved a few times from its original location. It is now in the old railroad depot, beside Hanover Creek. Yet mining did not begin in earnest until decades later, and Hanover still lies in the shadow of the massive Empire Zinc Company headframe, built during World War I. From then through to World War II, and on into the Cold War, zinc was Hanover's bread and butter. Then, in the fall of 1950, things got volatile, bringing outside attention to the remote little town.

For some time, Hispanic miners had been angry that the Empire Zinc Company, a subsidiary of the New Jersey Zinc Company, paid Anglos more for doing the

Hanover, NM, was the site of an infamous miner's strike in 1950.

same work, officially known as "dual wage rates." Hispanics were also the only ones given the more dangerous underground duties and were assigned the lowest quality company housing. So, on October 17, 1950, 140 miners walked off the job. These were members of the International Union of Mine, Mill, and Smelter Workers, whose leadership was suspected of being communist. Then eight months passed.

On that eighth month, the strike got even more intense. That is when the New Jersey Zinc Company hired strikebreakers and a federal judge issued a restraining order prohibiting further picketing by miners. At that point, the miners' wives and children took over picketing. As they were not miners, this was technically not a violation of the restraining order. It is said the local sheriff was quickly confronted with a "horde of screaming, singing, chanting women and children." Sixty-two of these women and children, including a one-month-old baby, were jailed until evening on the first day.

The miners' families continued picketing for another seven months. One wife of a miner said: "Everybody had a gun, except us. We had knitting needles. We had safety pins. We had straight pins. We had chile peppers. And we had rotten eggs." The strike ended fifteen months after it began, in January 1952, with miners receiving a modest wage increase along with life insurance, health benefits, and hot running water in their company homes.

Right: This silent headframe casts a shadow over Hanover.

Below: The vegetation enshrouded former home of the Hanover Post Office.

The whole episode resulted in a movie, *Salt of the Earth*, released in 1954. In the film, Hanover's name was changed to "Zinctown," and no shooting was done in the real Hanover, although some scenes were filmed in Fierro. Actual mine workers played roles similar to those they had had in real life, carrying side arms to protect themselves while doing so. That was because the film was written, directed, and produced by members of the Hollywood Ten, a group blacklisted for refusing to testify before the House Un-American Activities Committee (HUAC). For many years, it was almost impossible to actually see the movie due to its perceived communist associations. Now, of course, it is not very hard at all as the entire thing is on YouTube.

It seems a little late in the day to argue about whether creeping communism played a somehow-insidious role in the strike in Hanover. Fifteen years later, the International Union of Mine, Mill, and Smelter Workers would merge with the United Steelworkers of America. Yet you can imagine that in the early 1950s, there was trouble. Nevertheless, in a shady little corner of a rarely used bridge at the southern end of Hanover, there is a plaque dedicated by the Board of Grant County Commissioners, Armando D. Galindo, Conn W. Brown, and Zeke P. Santa Maria, which reads:

Villas Dry Goods Store No. 2 in Hanover: "Shoes Ready to Wear."

This bridge is dedicated to the memory of the Mine Mill Women's Auxiliary of 1951–1952. These brave women took over the picket line against the New Jersey Zinc Co. after their striking husbands were prohibited from picketing by an injunction. They were shot at, tear-gassed, run over and jailed but they stood strong in support of the International Union of Mine Mill and Smelter Workers.

We cannot leave Hanover without a quick mention of Villas Dry Goods Store No. 2, which used the slogan "Shoes Ready to Wear." The old false-front sits on a slight rise above Hanover, just before Fierro, in an area that may once have been a separate community known as Union Hill. You may ask where Villas Dry Goods Store No. 1 was—150 miles away in El Paso, naturally.

PEACE IN THE VALLEY: MONTICELLO

It is true that Monticello, New Mexico, like so many of the state's now-quieter places, is not a full-on ghost town. Some folks do indeed live here. However, it has got its fair share of old, empty structures, including an impressive adobe school built by the WPA. In 1980, Philip Varney included Monticello in *New Mexico's Best Ghost Towns: A Practical Guide* because of its "extraordinary charm." Well, perhaps not much has changed over a few decades because Monticello remains extraordinarily charming. Judging from Varney's photos, some buildings look better and some perhaps worse. However, if you stop for a couple of hours to eat lunch on the shady steps of the school and listen to the birds sing while the wind blows gently through the tall cottonwoods as I did, and then explore the rustic little plaza, you might think about buying a secluded retreat in Monticello, as I also did.

Monticello is 25 miles northwest of Truth or Consequences, not far from Cuchillo, and was originally founded in 1856 as Cañada Alamosa. The name honored the town's cottonwood-lined canyon. The Alamosa River flows alongside. Clearly, in the green, 23-mile-long Monticello Valley within which the town sits, cottonwood trees have always been a big deal.

Four years earlier, this location had become the headquarters of the Southern Apache Agency, and by 1870, around 500 Apaches lived in the area. However, in 1874, the agency for the Warm Springs band was moved a short distance to the northwest, to the Ojo Caliente Reservation, near present-day Dusty, in what is now known as the Monticello Box Canyon. In 1877, Geronimo was captured at Ojo Caliente by John Clum, the agency closed, and the Warm Springs band forcibly removed to the San Carlos Reservation in Arizona.

The Montoya home in Monticello, NM, holds many stories.

Monticello is not a true ghost town, but it is fun to make it look like one.

In 2003's *Ghost Towns Alive*, Linda Harris says Cañada Alamosa's official name change was the result of postal system bureaucracy. The story goes that in 1892 Alphonse Bourguet and his brother, Aristide, French emigrants, wanted to establish a post office in Cañada Alamosa. However, the policy of the day dictated that postal names be a single word. Alphonse had once been postmaster in Monticello, NY, and Aristide must have figured that name had worked well enough in New York because he submitted "Monticello" as Cañada Alamosa's replacement. This is all similarly recounted in Robert Julyan's *The Place Names of New Mexico*.

However, I have read other accounts, including in *New Mexico's Best Ghost Towns*, stating that John Sullivan was the first postmaster, also from Monticello, NY, and he made the change. I think this is now mostly considered incorrect. Whatever his role, John Sullivan's home was reportedly a stage stop, claimed to be the first in rugged Sierra County. Sullivan's place still stands off Highway 142, which leads into town and passes the plaza.

The Monticello Valley has always been a ranching and farming community, and it remains so today, producing organic vegetables and award-winning balsamic vinegar. Yet it is certainly true that it is not as bustling as in the past. The large Monticello Public School, mentioned earlier, stands as a picturesque shell. Built in 1935, one legend asserts that the school burned down when a student's chemistry experiment exploded. However, that is not true. The plaza, quiet and empty during my visit, once provided a thick-walled adobe fortress complete with gun holes to guard against Apache attacks. A couple homes on the outskirts of town are long-empty, with vintage vehicles parked outside in various degrees of decay. Of course, I was in heaven.

On the other hand, the San Ignacio Catholic Church, built in 1867, is well-maintained and lovely. Located on the north side of the plaza, services are still held here. There may yet be a dried-out pump organ in the choir loft. Restored territorial-style homes with corrugated tin roofs peek from behind lush greenery. What appears to have once been an antique store sits silently to the east of the plaza. Quite derelict in a photo in Varney's book, it has clearly been restored, even if it is now vacant again. Within its cool, blue walls are many antiques that might have once been for sale, and the ceiling shows several large, beautiful vigas running lengthwise. Outside are a low, weathered, wooden patio and an old bench.

In 1910, at its peak, Monticello had 573 residents, and there may have once been more than 1,000 families throughout the valley, which includes the adjacent village of Placita. The 2012 census has the population at 135, yet most folks probably do not live here year-round. I saw only a few people, all of whom passed by in cars or trucks as I took photos along the roadside.

Built in 1935, only the skeleton of the Monticello Public School remains.

I attempted to get to the cemetery southwest of the plaza, but after crossing the shallow Alamosa River, I ran into several private property signs without a graveyard in sight. I was lost yet again. It is a shame because I hate to miss an old cemetery. Yet it does provide an excuse for a return visit—as if I needed an excuse. To further prove that point, as I left Monticello four cow ponies crested the rise beside some abandoned cars—extraordinarily charming indeed.

HARD ROADS: ENGLE

There has not been much written about Engle, New Mexico. The usual ghost town books I consult only mention the town in the context of its stage and rail connections to other places, but Engle, now not much more than a handful of buildings persisting in the relentless heat of a dusty former rail stop slightly east of Truth or Consequences, sits within an area that has played a major role in the histories of Spain, Mexico, and the United States. Currently, it is the home base for a ranching enterprise owned by a well-known cable television magnate, and in the

Countless people have traveled through the landscape surrounding Engle, NM, over the centuries.

uncertain future, it may yet be passed through by some other very wealthy people on their way to orbit.

It makes sense to start the story of Engle with the *Jornada del Muerto* ("Journey of the Dead Man") which runs through the town or perhaps a couple hundred feet west, if you want to get technical. Considered the most treacherous part of *El Camino Real de Tierra Adentro* ("The Royal Road of the Interior Land" a.k.a. *El Camino Real*), this stretch, beginning slightly north of Las Cruces, traversed a desolate wasteland devoid of water, firewood, or shelter. So, if the Apache did not get you, the desert itself might. Just imagine traveling over an ancient lava bed by horse in the early 1600s without a Walmart or 7-11 in sight. It might sound like heaven now but let us not romanticize too much. The closest city to the north, a long 90 miles away, was named Socorro (i.e. succor, relief, aid, etc.) for a reason. Yet, all that aside, plenty of travelers did survive the journey and thus, for many years, one of the most important trade routes in the history of the world passed right outside what would become Engle's front door.

Founded in 1879, Engle is yet another western town of the railroad. Named for R. L. Engle, the railroad engineer who supervised construction of the line through here, due

Like so many New Mexico towns, Engle was born of the railroad.

to a paperwork error, Engle was officially known as "Angle" for its first six months. An attempt to rename the town "Engel" in the 1920s, in honor of AT&SF vice-president Edward J. Engel, was halted in the eleventh hour when "cowboy chronicler" Eugene Manlove Rhodes asked Senator Bronson Cutting to pull some strings.

The railroad soon built a station and Engle thrived as a shipping point for cattle from surrounding ranches. Horses, mules, stagecoaches, and eventually trains transported ore east from the more remote mining towns on the edge of the Black Range, including Cuchillo, Chloride, and Winston (then known as Fairview), and from Engle, it all moved on to larger cities, such as El Paso. A post office opened in 1881 and the place was off and running.

From 1911–1916, construction of Elephant Butte Dam, about 10 miles west, increased the population greatly. Housing in Engle was convenient, and the town was the switching point for the AT&SF spur that carried materials to the dam. The peak at that time was about 500 residents, but with completion of the dam workers left immediately and Engle began its decline. By 1919, 300 people, over half the peak population, had left. Seven years later, only seventy-five souls remained. In 1945, much of the land to the east and south was claimed by the federal government for White Sands Missile Range, snuffing out most of Engle's remaining light, but not quite all of it.

While the post office closed in 1955, a few people live in Engle yet. The train still rumbles by; it just does not stop anymore. Not many original buildings stand, but one, the old schoolhouse, occupies what would seem to be the spiritual center of town. That is not just on account of it being the most prominent building you see as you cross the railroad tracks, but because it is now the Engle Country Church featuring "bible preaching and gospel singing" every so often. Conveniently, there are some vineyards being tended nearby, too, in case the supply of wine runs low.

Engle has become the headquarters of the Armendaris Ranch, a massive 362,885-acre spread owned by Ted Turner of CNN and Jane Fonda fame. Word is that when he comes to town his entourage lays the necessary groundwork a few days in advance and then Ted blows in, checks on his buffalo, maybe does a little hunting, and is off again. Turner owns two other huge ranches in New Mexico and is one of the largest private landowners in the state.

Moving into the surreal, Engle is still perhaps poised to be a way station for those heading to the much-beleaguered Spaceport America. Anyone not flying directly into and out of the spaceport or coming up from Las Cruces would be obliged to go through Engle. It is strange to imagine that some of the richest, most famous people on the planet could see lonely Engle shortly before they are launched into orbit for a few seconds. On the other hand, those who traveled the *Jornada del Muerto* hundreds of years ago might well appreciate the irony as the dusty little patch of Chihuahuan Desert on which Engle abides has a habit of being a quiet witness to great journeys.

"Bible preaching and gospel singing" still occurs at the Engle Country Church.

PAT GARRETT REALLY SHOULD HAVE STAYED THE NIGHT: ORGAN

Organ, New Mexico, is—believe it or not—another not-total-ghost town that I am going to make look like one. Sorry, good people of Organ; I will explain in a minute.

Organ is named for the razor-spired Organ Mountains visible to the south, which themselves were so-named because they look like the pipes of an organ. Originating as a mining encampment in the 1840s, the town was officially founded in 1883 as lead, copper, fluorite, zinc, gold, and silver mines were punched into the hill slopes to the northeast with ever-increasing frequency. By the turn of the century, Organ was peaking at perhaps 1,800 residents, and may have had any or all of seven saloons, two smelters, two general stores, a two-teacher school, a Catholic church, a post office, a hotel, and a jail in a tunnel that had once been a powder magazine.

It may seem strange that Organ was not called San Augustin in honor of the San Augustin Mountains immediately to the northeast, or 7,030-foot San Augustin Peak, which literally towers over the town to the east, or even San Augustin Pass, now part of U.S. Highway 70/82, which, if traveled eastward, will take you down into the vast Tularosa Basin and the southern extent of the White Sands Missile Range. In 1908, long before U.S. 70/82 had a name, it was on this same stretch of road, traveling southwestward toward Las Cruces, that Sheriff Pat Garrett was shot and killed some twenty-eight years after he had shot Billy the Kid in Fort Sumner. This bit of Organ's history has remained long after its mines, which filled with water in the 1930s, have mostly faded from memory.

As Organ is the closest inhabited place to the missile range, it was revived some-what in the mid-1940s when work began on the atomic bomb and missile range employees moved in. Thus, while the population is still only just over 300, there are many well-kept homes. Philip Varney mentions Bentley's Store and Assay Office in *New Mexico's Best Ghost Towns* and notes that it had become a private residence. This is still true, and in fact, the old building looks to be very well-maintained with lots of tended greenery out front. Varney also mentions the Organ School, notable for its corner bell tower, but I missed it. The tower has been removed and the school now seemingly blends right in with its neighbors.

So, you may ask, if there are a few hundred people living in Organ, renovating their historic homes, why the photos of derelict buildings? Well, the ruins are on the south side of the highway. Those are the Organ Mountains behind the lodge. As to why virtually every commercial enterprise on that side of the road has been abandoned and apparently long-abandoned, I cannot say. Perhaps people prefer to eat and shop in Las Cruces, 15 miles away. That is really the only other commercial district in the area, but as New Mexico's second-largest city, it would certainly offer

Above left: Stop by Organ, NM for a "spooky sandwitch [*sic.*]".

Above right: The Slumbering Mountain Cemetery is still accepting new residents.

The Organ Mountains beckon in the distance beyond Organ, New Mexico.

some retail competition. Whatever the case, I find it surprising that the spectacular views of the Organ Mountains to the south, San Augustin Peak to the east and Las Cruces to the southwest haven't had more people stopping for "sandwitches [*sic.*]." I know I would stop for a bite.

TROUBLED TIMES: STEINS

Steins (pronounced "steens"), New Mexico, is a ghost town whose recent history is as violent and troubled as its distant past. In *New Mexico's Best Ghost Towns*, Philip Varney starts the tale in 1873 with Captain Enoch Steens, a member of the US Cavalry who fought a battle against Apaches in Doubtful Canyon, not far from what is now the New Mexico–Arizona border. The canyon's sobriquet reflected the view of most settlers on their odds of traveling through the place without getting killed. The story goes that Captain Steens could not do it either and the site of his supposed death was later known as Steins [*sic.*] Peak. However, in *Ghost Towns Alive: Trips to New Mexico's Past*, Linda Harris says that Major (he had been promoted) Enoch Steens merely camped in the area in 1856, rumors of his death being greatly exaggerated as he lived until 1880. I think Ms. Harris has it right. Incidentally, Steens is referred to as Samuel Chamberlain's captain (Company "E," First U.S. Dragoons) in Chamberlain's somewhat exaggerated autobiography, *My Confession: The Recollections of a Rogue*, the main source material for Cormac McCarthy's *Blood Meridian*. This would have been 1846, during the Mexican–American War, a decade before Steens camped near Doubtful Canyon.

In 1880, the Southern Pacific Railroad came through this gap in the Peloncillo Mountains, then-known as Steins Pass. The name was misspelled thanks to the Butterfield Overland Mail Route, which, back in 1858, had christened their Doubtful Canyon stagecoach stop, about eight miles to the northwest, Steins Peak Station. In 1888, a post office was established, and in 1905, about the time the Southern Pacific's rock crushing operation began, the "Pass" was dropped, and the place became simply "Steins," still pronounced like Major Enoch's name.

Varney states that the post office was established at Doubtful Canyon and moved to Steins. However, although it was on the mail route, there was never a PO at Steins Peak Station. Robert Julyan's *The Place Names of New Mexico* does a nice job of clearing up the confusion surrounding Steins Peak Station, Steins Peak, and Steins Pass (and Steins Mountain, almost two miles northwest of Steins and therefore not where you would find Steins Peak).

Steins, NM, has seen its share of troubled times.

Steins surroundings are rugged, desolate, and changeless.

The town's population hit 100, and all modern conveniences were available, except water, which came only from Doubtful Canyon or, even more rarely, the sky. There was a dance hall, a two-story hotel, a saloon, and a two-room brothel. That is one demimondaine for every fifty residents. I honestly do not know if that is a better or worse ratio than would be expected.

When the Southern Pacific were here crushing gravel for 300 miles of rail bed, the Chinese who did the work were not allowed to live in Steins; they had to stay out by the quarry itself. Incidentally, the ground of the cemetery, now south of Interstate 10, was reportedly so hard that graves had to be blasted out of the earth; maybe things were kind of tough. Even now, if you go to Steins in the summer, it can feel like the sun is trying to roast you.

The quarry was shuttered in the 1920s and that would be Steins peak, population 200—again, not to be confused with Steins Peak (elevation 5,715 feet). From there, it was downhill, although the railroad station operated until 1950, when it was moved to Cottonwood City, just to the south. The post office had left six years earlier. Then Steins languished for years, many of its buildings burning down in a 1962 fire. Philip Varney's photo from the 1970s makes it look like by then hardly anything remained besides some crumbling adobes. For some years, a man named Warren Garrison lived there alone, his family having bought the town site for him. He has said: "It was the dream of a lifetime to end up there in '76 with the clothes on my back, a sleeping bag, my little dog Spooky and $9 in my pocket."

In 1988, Steins was purchased by Larry and Linda Link, who restored some buildings and gathered artifacts from the surrounding community. They then opened Steins as a tourist attraction. At one point, the town attracted 90,000 visitors a year, but vandalism and theft had gotten so bad by 2008 that the Links were forced to allow Steins to become a *bona fide* ghost town for the second time.

The following year, when I first saw Steins, the little ghost town was entirely closed-off. Very un-ghostly semi-trailers with "FUMIGATION" painted in big, red letters on their sides were parked around the perimeter. Signs warning of methyl bromide hung on the fences. This was interesting as the use of methyl bromide, an ozone-depleting pesticide, was phased out in 2005. It was unclear what was going on, but it seemed that I would not be seeing Steins up close.

Then, on June 7, 2011, the story took a more tragic turn. Steins is only a few yards from I-10, and very early that morning someone probably exited off the interstate for reasons still unknown. It is likely that Larry Link, suffering from insomnia, went to have a look. He was shot five times. Presumably, the shooter then drove away, leaving an untraceable gun behind. Early reports portrayed Link as a rancher and his assailant as a migrant coming up from the Mexican border,

Deadly poison is not what one typically hopes to encounter in a ghost town.

less than 40 miles away. Such inaccuracy and politicized speculation angered the Link family.

In spring 2013, Linda Link and her granddaughter re-opened Steins, but before I could get down to have a look, it was closed again. However, the Steins Facebook page would seem to indicate that tours of the town may again be occurring on a semi-regular schedule.

Later, I learned the Link family had at one time been applying pesticide to produce coming through on I-10. Whether they were still using methyl bromide or just got a deal on outdated signs, I cannot say. As for Larry Link's killer, that mystery has been harder to solve. To date, police have confirmed just a single lead in the case. There have been no arrests.

7

THE OLD NEW MEXICO STATE PENITENTIARY

S anta Fe is the oldest capital city in the country, founded in 1610 by Spanish colonists after a few years of initial habitation. In fact, it is the oldest European community west of the Mississippi River. It can be an indescribably charming place after a chile-fueled meal, the smell of piñon heavy in the air, but it has occasionally been something else, as well.

PENITENTIARY BLUES: THE SANTA FE PRISON RIOT

Some 15 miles south of Santa Fe stands the old New Mexico State Penitentiary, which opened in 1956 and closed in 1998. Virtually every other piece of historical information regarding the prison pales into insignificance in the face of a riot which began at approximately 2 a.m. on February 2, 1980. That riot is considered to be the most violent prison uprising in U.S. history (though not the deadliest; that dubious honor likely goes to the 1971 riot at Attica in New York). Information on the prison's architecture and overall history apart from the riot is buried under the mountain of horror unleashed that day in February. So, here is the story of the New Mexico State Penitentiary riot.

In the early 1970s, the New Mexico State Penitentiary operated under a system whereby certain inmates were selected to help run prison programs. These prisoners could approve or reject other prisoner's requests to join programs, and as these programs were popular with the prisoners, it was in everyone's best interest to assure their continuance. Thus, the selected inmates, in cooperation with their fellow prisoners, made sure that order was maintained, and no one jeopardized their good thing.

The gas chamber in the old New Mexico State Penitentiary was used just once, in 1960.

However, by the late 1970s, the New Mexico correctional system was in disarray. The chain of command among prison officials was weak and confusing and oversight of regulations lax. Around this time, prisoner-led programs ended, and a new policy was implemented, one whereby prisoners were routinely turned against each other and coercion was used to obtain information and overall compliance. "Divide and conquer" became the guiding objective.

Furthermore, the New Mexico State Penitentiary contained high-security cells, New Mexico's death row, and its attendant gas chamber, as well as the protective custody unit, where inmates considered at risk of assault in the general population were housed. This included prisoners who had given evidence against their fellow inmates. The prison, when built in 1956, was designed to contain 800 men, but by 1980, more than 1,100 prisoners lived together in close quarters. The renovation of a cellblock around this time saw some of the most dangerous criminals moved from a high-security area to dormitory-style housing. This overcrowding and mixing of New Mexico's most violent, notorious, disturbed, and vulnerable lawbreakers in one facility was more fuel to be tossed on what was already becoming a dangerous powder keg.

Finally, those guarding the inmates at the penitentiary had grown demoralized and careless. In any given year, 80 percent of the prison staff quit. The high turnover rate meant that guards were frequently unfamiliar with the operation of the prison and the building itself, nor would the guards always know the history of those incarcerated. At the time of the riot, many guards let prisoners do as they pleased in their cells, as long as it did not turn into something the guards had to deal with personally.

A typical cell block.

Thus many prisoners were routinely victims of physical and sexual assault, and drug use was rampant. In addition to drugs, some prisoners made their own alcohol, which ended up being the flame which finally lit the fuse on the powder keg.

While on their rounds during the early morning of February 2, two guards came upon a couple of prisoners in a dormitory that were drunk on alcohol they had made with fermented fruit. The intoxicated inmates attacked and overcame the guards, and as the guards had failed to follow procedure, leaving the cell block doors they had just come through open, the prisoners quickly made their way to the prison's control center, where they flipped switches unlocking most of the penitentiary. Once free, hundreds of inmates fanned throughout the prison, taking fourteen guards and one medical technician hostage. While things were about to get much worse, some inmates were already fighting the tide; three guards were given safe hiding places by sympathetic prisoners. Meanwhile, anything that could be used as a weapon was procured and made into one, and the hospital was raided for its drug supply. Even glue was sought out and huffed.

It was about this time that some inmates, possibly less than a dozen, set out for the protective custody unit. Once there, suspected informers were taken from their cells and set on fire or had their limbs cut off one-by-one, each successive wound cauterized to prolong the suffering. One prisoner was propped in front of a window, in full view of the National Guard, now gathered beyond the 12-foot fence outside, and killed with a blowtorch. While keys to the outside doors of several wings of the prison were available, the decision was made not to enter and, instead, to attempt to negotiate with the prisoners. Meanwhile, the carnage inside escalated.

During the negotiations, it became clear that, in fact, no one was in charge of the riot, and therefore, no one was in a position to negotiate to stop it. Those convicts communicating with the outside made claims of overcrowding, bad food, and harassment. Others, weary of the violence, began to leave the prison and line up along the outside fence, seeking refuge. Other prisoners tried to protect certain of their fellow inmates and lost their lives because of it. Still others worked to release the guards. Such was the disarray that prisoners released hostages as their fellow inmates made demands intended to be met before those very same hostages would be released.

By the bitter end, only three hostages remained and two very violent prisoners—Michael Colby and William Jack Stephens—demanded and were granted transfer to a federal facility in exchange for the hostage's release. Colby and Stephens were told to get their belongings from their cells, and the State Police and the National Guard entered the prison and retook it without opposition from the approximately 100 inmates still inside.

Those entering the prison found true horror: bodies had been put in ovens in the kitchen, limbs were scattered on the ground, one corpse had no head, another was hanging from the ceiling with the word "RAT" cut into the chest, and yet another

Above left: A group of cells adjacent to death row.

Above right: Regulations regarding graffiti in cells were relaxed shortly before the penitentiary closed.

131

had a metal bar shoved in one ear and out the other. The bodies of two inmates were never found and presumed entirely incinerated. All told, the thirty-six-hour nightmare left at least thirty-three inmates dead and nine badly injured. One guard was in very serious condition while other guards were badly beaten and sodomized; the New Mexico Corrections Department had been brought to its knees.

The causes of the riot were all preventable. Lawsuits had already been filed regarding the overcrowding; the lack of a command structure within the NM prison system was well-known (basic security inspections at the penitentiary went undone for years because no one knew who should be performing them); and the use of drugs among inmates was no secret. Therefore, the riot itself should have come as no surprise. What is surprising, of course, is the level of violence. Obviously, housing the protective custody unit, which included "snitches," in the main facility was a grievous mistake and one subsequently corrected. Yet, beyond that, and in overpowering opposition to those inmates (possibly the vast majority) who did not participate or even risked and lost their lives to reduce the violence, something unspeakably wicked was at work over those thirty-six hours. James Weston, the chief medical examiner at the time, was quoted as saying, "Virtually every one of the bodies had overkill, which is to say that there was more than mob hysteria. There was rage." That much seems abundantly clear, but the prison psychologist, Dr. Marc Orner, made a much more telling statement when he said:

> None of us really understands what happened in there. The depth of the violence is incomprehensible to me as a human being and as a psychologist. It is as if all the aggression a human being can have was savagely unleashed. We just can't understand why they did this to each other.

Interestingly enough, apart from changes to the prison system in the years following the riot, changes in the prison population itself have reduced the likelihood of such riots. Prison gangs have consolidated their power, and where numerous small gangs used to fight for position and influence, now only a couple of well-established gangs maintain a fragile peace. Finally, in the mid-1980s, drug smuggling within the New Mexico State Penitentiary (and, I would imagine, prisons throughout the country) became more sophisticated and materially lucrative. Drugs are now a significant incentive, both to the users and distributors within prisons, and no one wants to rock the boat if it means they might not get their fix. In this way, crime controls the criminal.

8

NORTHEASTERN NEW MEXICO

The first photographs I ever took in New Mexico were in the northeastern portion of the state—including the historic city of Clayton and Cimarron's authentically Wild West St. James Hotel—and the region will always hold a special place in my heart. It could be lawless and violent, with more than its share of duplicity and bloodshed, but it is somewhat less intimidating now than it must have been in those storied days of train robberies and land wars.

In the High Country: Elizabethtown

Elizabethtown is just north of Eagle Nest, on the "Loop of Enchantment," not too far from the Colorado border. Fairly well-known as far as ghost towns go, there is even a sporadically open museum on-site. However, there is not much left of the place, and it is yet another New Mexico ghost town that came into (and out of) existence because of shiny rocks. In 1866, Captain John William Moore helped a wounded Native American get medical attention at Fort Union, near Las Vegas, New Mexico. Once recovered, the man returned to Fort Union to trade and ran into Captain Moore, whose previous kindness he now repaid with a few decorative stones that Mr. Moore immediately realized bore copper. Moore asked to be taken to the source of the rocks, which turned out to be high on 12,441-foot Mt. Baldy, just across the Moreno Valley from Wheeler Peak, which, at over 13,161 feet, is the highest point in New Mexico. Even better than copper, it turned out that the mountains and valleys were rich with gold, and so another western gold boom began.

Elizabethtown, named after Captain Moore's young daughter, became the first officially incorporated town in the state, and a post office opened before 1866 was out. By the time Elizabethtown celebrated its first birthday, the population had ballooned

A 1946 Mercury is poised to enjoy the view from Elizabethtown, NM, for all eternity.

to 3,000, 5,000, or maybe 7,000. No one really seems to know for sure, but a lot of people showed up in a short period. Just before 1870, E-town, as miners referred to it, reputedly boasted over 100 buildings, including a couple of hotels, seven saloons (some said to be 200 feet long), three dance halls, and a drugstore. However, as is a theme in the Wild West, not all of that is necessarily true. *Caveat emptor.*

You do not have to dig too deep into a town's past to find something unsavory, and Elizabethtown is no exception. In late 1870, the Ute wife of Charles Kennedy, who lived on the road between E-town and Taos, entered a saloon bleeding and crying. She told those gathered that her husband had been killing travelers. Depending on whom you believe, he may have murdered up to fourteen people and might even have killed two of his own children after they got on his nerves. Whatever the case, the last of his kids truly did raise the old man's ire when Kennedy lured a traveler into his home only to have the man ask if there were any Indians in the area. Kennedy's son is said to have replied, "Can't you smell the one papa put under the floor?" This retort displeased the boy's father so much that he shot the traveler immediately and then bashed his son's head against the fireplace. After that, he threw the bodies in the cellar, locked his wife up, and started drinking. Eventually, he drank so much that his wife was able to escape up the chimney.

Kennedy was arrested and a trial (or pre-trial) held in which a young lawyer named Melvin Whitson Mills either was going to buy Kennedy's freedom or had already secured a hung jury. Reports vary. In any case, as seems to have happened fairly often in the Wild West, exoneration was sensed, and a mob quickly formed and dragged Kennedy from jail. The mob was led by the notorious (and dangerous) Clay Allison, and Kennedy was summarily taken back to Elizabethtown and dragged through the streets with a noose around his neck for a very long time.

This is often considered to be Froelick's Store, which survived a major fire. If true, while slightly modified, this would be the only original building left intact in E-town.

It is sometimes said this is the ruin of the Mutz Hotel, but that may not be true.

It has been said that Allison removed Kennedy's head and gave it to Henri Lambert, owner of the Lambert Inn (later the St. James Hotel) in Cimarron, now considered one of the most haunted hotels in the country. Lambert apparently was told to hang the head outside his establishment as a warning and it eventually mummified on the corral fence before finally disappearing. Yet as much as I like stories about the St. James Hotel, Lambert would have actually been living in E-town, not Cimarron, if Kennedy was killed in 1870. Could the head have been placed outside Lambert's Elizabethtown saloon then and not taken to Cimarron at all? Could Kennedy's death have occurred after 1870? Is there a primary source that can be found to straighten all this out? Not that I have seen yet, and it sure would be nice to see the original documents from Kennedy's arrest and trial, should they exist, which they may well not.

Even aside from the Kennedy affair, E-town was a notoriously rough place. When one defendant asked to be tried in a different city because he figured he could not get a fair trial in Elizabethtown, some citizens just took the man from the sheriff themselves and hanged him, pinning a note to his coat that read, "So much for change of venue."

By 1875, Elizabethtown was basically abandoned, but the AT&SF Railroad (and the newfound ability to both transport ore long distances and commence dredging operations) brought the town back to life. E-town also became a musical hotspot, with people traveling from all around to hear fiddle playing on a Saturday night.

In 1903, Remsberg's Store went up in flames and a large part of the town went with it. Dredging operations ended in 1905 and E-town's massive dredger, named *Eleanor*, was left to sink deeper into Moreno Creek with each passing year. It is still in the creek, but entirely buried now. Then it was a long, slow fade until 1917 or so, by which time hardly anyone was left in E-town. The post office hung on until 1931.

As I said, there is not a whole lot to see nowadays—aside from the spectacular natural surroundings, that is. There are the large remains of what was a two-story building, which some say was the Mutz Hotel. However, Ofelia Barber, who was married in the building in 1872, stated that it was not the Mutz, but another facility, supposedly with rooms to rent on the first floor and a dance hall on the second. Judging by other photos, even this ruin is a shadow of what it was less than twenty years ago. The Elizabethtown Cemetery seems to still be quite active, and not surprisingly. Who would not want their final resting place to be on a hill overlooking the Moreno Valley, with Mt. Baldy to the east and Wheeler Peak to the west? Mrs. Barber left not only her husband but two daughters in this cemetery when she moved from E-town in 1936, one of its very last remaining residents.

A resting place with a view in Elizabethtown.

The St. James Hotel in Cimarron, NM, as I first saw it in late 2005.

WE'LL SHOOT THE LIGHTS OUT FOR YOU: THE ST. JAMES HOTEL, CIMARRON

In the fall of 2005, I was driving from Oklahoma to Taos via U.S. 64 and, on a whim, stopped for a few minutes at the St. James Hotel in Cimarron, New Mexico. I immediately knew I wanted to spend some time there, but the road was calling and soon I had to be on my way. I bid the place adieu and vowed to return. Back then, I did not know that the St. James is considered one of the most haunted hotels in the United States. All I knew was what I had just read in an article tacked to a wall; that the hotel began operating in 1872, that twenty-six people had been killed in the saloon alone, and that everyone from Jesse James and Buffalo Bill to Clay Allison and Zane Grey had spent the night. As it turns out, not quite all of those claims are necessarily true, but the St. James still stands as one of the premier Wild West hotels.

In the previous section, on the ghost town of Elizabethtown, I mention Henri Lambert. Lambert, a Frenchman, had moved from Petersburg, Virginia to Elizabethtown in late 1868 to try his luck at mining. Eventually, he gave up on gold, however, and returned to his previous occupation as a chef. It has been said that Lambert was Abraham Lincoln's personal cook, but there is no hard evidence. On the other hand, it may be is true that Lambert was once presented with a severed head. More on that grim tale can be found in the history of Elizabethtown.

Lambert left E-town in 1871, moved to Cimarron (Spanish for "feral," but also meaning "wild" or "fugitive"), and in late 1871, he opened a saloon, which became known as Lambert's Place. Not surprisingly, the saloon did a brisk business, and by 1882, Lambert had added hotel rooms and a restaurant. Lambert's Place became the Lambert Inn, one of the finest hotels in the territory, and, eventually, was renamed the St. James Hotel.

Cimarron was indeed a wild place and some people certainly met their fate in or around the hotel between 1872 and 1884. Henri Lambert himself killed a man, although the death was due to the deceased, Juan Benito Archuleta, falling and striking his head on the saloon's fireplace. By the mid-1870s, legend has it that it was not uncommon to be asked, "Who was killed at Lambert's last night?" Yet it may not have been that wild. Notorious Texas gunfighter, rancher, and outlaw Clay Allison is considered to have killed the most people at the St. James, credited with two and perhaps three murders. Given the reputation of Mr. Allison, that figure seems fairly modest. Still, numerous bullet holes remain in the saloon's tin ceiling to bear witness to rough and rowdy times.

If you believe what has been written, you would think that many—if not most—of the major figures of the Wild West stayed at the St. James Hotel, and you know, that

Right: You may just hear the footsteps of Buffalo Bill and Doc Holliday echo down these halls.

Below: Many of the Wild West's most colorful characters checked into the St. James.

could just about be true. Yet first, it is said that Jesse James stayed at the hotel, and that may well not be true. There is no hard evidence he ever came farther north than Las Vegas, NM (with that only recorded as an apocryphal meeting with Billy the Kid), if he was ever in the state at all. Annie Oakley appears in a list of undated names reportedly hand-copied by Fred Lambert, Henri's son, from the hotel's 1872–1885 registers (the originals through 1880 have since disappeared; the rest went to Oklahoma) along with other members of the Wild West Show, including Buffalo Bill Cody. Annie would have just been joining the show by 1885, while Buffalo Bill is said to have gone on to become a personal friend of the Lambert's. Clay Allison most certainly stayed many times, leaving some bodies behind to prove it.

Bob Ford, the guy who shot Jesse James, appears in the register, too. Ford is sometimes credited with shooting a man named Bill Curren in the St. James in 1882, the same year he shot Jesse, although he may not have actually killed Bill. After all, there had been a poker game earlier that night that also included Dick Liddil, one of the last men left standing from the James-Younger Gang.

Other figures like Black Jack Ketchum, Wyatt Earp, and Doc Holliday were also there. Fred Lambert noted that the entire Black Jack Ketchum Gang stayed in the 1890s under assumed names. Wyatt Earp, his brother James, their wives, and Doc Holliday would have been right on the front doorstep of the hotel while traveling the Mountain Route of the Santa Fe Trail to Las Vegas, NM, in 1879. In the early twentieth century, Zane Grey definitely spent time at the hotel, writing some of *Fighting Caravans* in room twenty-two.

History continues to be made at the St. James Hotel.

It is useful to know who really stayed at the St. James Hotel so that, in the event of a haunting, you can better guess whose ghost you are dealing with. So Jesse James is not likely, but Henri's first wife, Mary Stepp Lambert, who died in the east wing in 1881, is possible if you are in room seventeen and there is suddenly an overpowering scent of rose perfume. However, the most interesting spectral figure at the St. James may be Thomas James (T. J.) Wright, who was reportedly killed upstairs in the hallway following an evening of gambling. One story has Lambert himself shooting Wright in the back as Wright walked away after Lambert had gambled (and lost) his entire hotel to T. J. That is almost certainly inaccurate, but whatever the case, Wright was dead at the age of twenty-two. Now Wright's violent spirit is said to occupy his old room: number eighteen. So many guests have reported being tormented by T. J's ghost—some claiming to have been physically hurt—that room eighteen is now padlocked and guests are not allowed inside. The bartender said that he sometimes goes up to the room and has a glass of whiskey, leaving one behind for Mr. Wright, as well.

I have to say I slept very well in room seventeen. In the morning, I peeked through a crack in the door to get a look at room eighteen. I could see some torn wallpaper with holes showing through the plaster and plenty of dust. Whatever is going on, that room has not been used for a while.

The St. James hit hard times when the railroad cut off traffic along the adjacent Santa Fe Trail and the mines began to close. The hotel was bought and sold many times, and by the mid-1980s, it had fallen into disrepair. Yet in 1985, the St. James was restored, and after some additional work, today it is in excellent vintage condition. You can also stay in the annex wing, built in the 1960s but still reportedly good and haunted, and dine at the large restaurant and bar. The old place is once again the liveliest thing going in Cimarron.

WHEN YOUR ROPE IS TOO LONG: CLAYTON

Clayton, New Mexico, is a little bit out of the way. You are probably not going to just suddenly stumble into it unless you are traveling through the wide-open landscape where New Mexico, Oklahoma, and Texas all meet, in which case, sure, maybe you will happen across this once bustling burg.

Despite its isolated location, Clayton is famous for several things. There are lots of dinosaur footprints nearby, and a volcano, too. The lovely Eklund Hotel is there, established in 1892 and once the finest railroad hotel between Fort Worth and Denver. There are even two bullet holes still visible in the tin ceiling of the old saloon; that is maybe not as impressive once you know the shots were fired by

The Eklund Hotel, built in 1892, is still the place to spend the night in Clayton, NM.

excited supporters of President Warren G. Harding upon his election in 1920. No injuries were reported. However, if you find a bullet in the wall, it might be from the early morning in 1909 when City Marshal Pete Barker, drunk and overeager for his gun, was killed by jailer Frank Garcia. However, Clayton was also the site of what is widely agreed to be the most botched hanging in the West, that of Thomas Edward "Black Jack" Ketchum. I looked into it all one frozen, windswept weekend before Thanksgiving while based at the Eklund.

Black Jack was born in Texas and began leaving a trail of alleged crime in 1890, at age twenty-seven, right around the time he came to New Mexico. Possibly a soured love affair drove him off the rails. If so, crime must have already been in his genes because his older brother, Sam, left his wife and family to become an outlaw, as well. I say Black Jack's crimes were "alleged" because while he was connected to many robberies and dark occurrences over the years, including the famous disappearance of politician Albert Jennings Fountain and his young son, Henry, near Las Cruces, he was never convicted of anything until being sentenced to death for attempting to rob a train. This was unusual as no one else in American history was ever executed for train robbery alone.

Eventually, Black Jack and his brother joined the loosely organized Hole in the Wall Gang in the north-central part of the state, sometimes making a living ranching and, at other times, jockeying for position with Butch Cassidy's Hole in the Wall-affiliated crew, the Wild Bunch.

On September 3, 1897, the Hole in the Wall Gang robbed a train between Folsom and Des Moines, NM. They did so again on July 11, 1899, but Black Jack did not participate in the second effort. After the second robbery, a gunfight ensued near

Agriculture continues to be dominant in northeastern NM, but its scale is diminished.

Yet another indication of agriculture's struggle amid a declining population.

Cimarron, and Sam was badly wounded. A second shoot-out occurred a few days later, and a sheriff and deputy were killed. Sam was finally caught but died a short time later of his injuries in the Santa Fe Territorial Prison.

On August 16, 1899, Black Jack attempted to single-handedly rob the same train, unaware that his brother was recently dead from a similar idea. Black Jack boarded the engine but may have forced it to stop on a sharp turn where the cars with the loot could not be uncoupled. Meanwhile, the conductor, Frank Harrington, and the mail agent were getting sick of being robbed and opened fire. Black Jack's right arm was nearly severed at the elbow by a double-barreled shotgun, but, switching his rifle to his left hand, he still managed to wound both Harrington and the agent. Black Jack then escaped into the night.

It is said that Black Jack laid out all night until "help" arrived in the form of another train, then raised his gun as the conductor and brakeman approached him. They offered to shoot him right then if he wanted a fight, but he replied, "No, boys, I am all done. Take me in." This may be apocryphal.

What is not apocryphal is that Black Jack's arm was amputated in Trinidad, Colorado, and then, restored to relative health, he was sent back to Clayton for trial. Convicted of "felonious assault upon a railway train," Black Jack became the only person sentenced to death under the law, which was later overturned by the Supreme Court as carrying too severe a sentence.

Now, Clayton had never seen a hanging before, and they were not quite sure what to do, besides sell tickets and tiny Black Jack dolls hanging from miniature stick gallows. The execution was delayed several times, but rumors of a plan to break Black Jack out of jail got a date finalized.

Meanwhile, Black Jack wrote a letter to President McKinley saying that innocent men were imprisoned for a robbery that Ketchum and his gang had committed at Steins Pass. Yet he maintained that he had never killed anyone and was a victim of mistaken identity, having been confused with another outlaw, Black Jack Christian, killed four years earlier. His last requests were music and female companionship. The former he received via violin and guitar; the latter was denied due to a lack of public funds with which to pay the companion. It was said that he did at least eat a hearty final dinner.

On April 26, 1901, after a further delay of several hours for continued fine-tuning of the gallows, Black Jack stood on the scaffold and these words are often said to have been his last: "I'll be in hell before you start breakfast, boys! Let her rip!"

Black Jack did say something like that, but not immediately before he dropped and not for just any "boys." The first part of the quotation appears in the *Santa Fe New Mexican*, dated April 26, 1901, the day of the hanging, and is directed toward Frank Harrington, the conductor who shot Black Jack's arm off. When Ketchum's

"Against this wall Thomas Edward 'Black Jack' Ketchum swung into eternity."

lawyer was leaving his cell for presumably the last time, Black Jack told him, "Say, tell Harrington I'll meet him in hell for breakfast."

This was after he had requested to "be buried face down so Harrington can kiss my ass." The next morning, according to the *New Mexican*, he told Sheriff Salome Garcia to "hurry up the hanging so he could get to hell in time for dinner."

The other part of the quotation comes from what truly were Black Jack's last words. Sheriff Garcia, apparently drunk, was having a hard time cutting the rope to open the gallows doors. The *New Mexican* records that Ketchum, nervous and impatient, said, "Let 'er go, boys. Let 'er go."

The *San Francisco Chronicle* reported that Black Jack was somewhat more subdued, his legs trembling, saying only, "Good-by. Please dig my grave very deep. All right; hurry up." Still other accounts have simply, "Hurry up, boys, get this over with."

Whatever he said, Black Jack clearly wanted it all done fast. The sheriff needed two swings of the hatchet to cut the rope, but the trap finally fell open and Black Jack dropped. However, the rope was too long and, possibly due to over-testing with a 200-pound sandbag, no longer had any elasticity. Thus, Black Jack was instantly decapitated, one of only three such occurrences over a few hundred years of recorded judicial hangings in the U.S. and Europe. Apparently, Ketchum's headless body landed on its feet and even remained upright for a moment, spurting blood. Sheriff John McCandlass, visiting from Dalhart, Texas, held the corpse to the ground to stop the convulsions that followed. Five minutes is reportedly how long Black Jack's heart continued beating, but who really knows? The *SF Chronicle* noted that the heart clearly continued beating for a while.

The cold grave of Thomas Ketchum.

Photos exist of the gruesome aftermath, the separated head still contained in the black hood and lying in front of the one-armed corpse. Then, in another strange twist, Black Jack's head was sewn back on his body before burial at 2.30 p.m. that day in Clayton's Boothill. One wonders how much effort they put into the job. No one was ever executed in all of Union County again.

Black Jack's grave was moved from the original Boothill to the current Clayton Cemetery in the 1930s. In the end, he got Shakespeare for an epitaph ("And How His Audit Stands, Who Knows Save Heaven") and still gets flowers over 100 years after his death. We should all be so lucky. When Black Jack was exhumed in 1933 to be moved to the new Clayton cemetery his coffin was opened and it was found that his request to be buried face down, too, had been denied. As a final addendum, Teddy Roosevelt was apparently presented with Black Jack's Winchester 30-30 for some reason that I cannot quite figure out.

Let Me Die at Home: The Melvin Mills Mansion, Springer

On the windswept plains of Northeastern New Mexico looms the disheveled yet still stately former home of Melvin Whitson Mills, a three-story adobe territorial mansion with more than twenty rooms, carved walnut features, and a massive cistern out back.

Melvin Mills died broken and penniless in the mansion he built in Springer, NM. Or did he?

Melvin Mills (or "Colonel," as he was known to friends) was born in 1845 in Ontario, Canada, his Quaker parents moving to Michigan shortly thereafter. He graduated from Ann Arbor Law School in 1869 and then came out to Elizabethtown, where a gold rush was in full swing. Yet Elizabethtown eventually began to founder, and Mills played a key role in getting the Colfax County Seat moved from there to a new town he was helping establish, this one named after Territorial attorney Frank Springer.

In 1877, Mills, both a district attorney and New Mexico territorial legislator, platted Springer with William Thornton and took up residence, building the magnificent mansion. It is considered the most unique architecture along the old Santa Fe Trail, two branches of which ran either side of Springer, coming together again about 50 miles south of town. East of Springer was the Cimarron Cutoff, close enough that perhaps the dust of wagons could be seen from the balcony of Mill's house on a clear day. To the west, and somewhat farther out, ran the Mountain Branch. It is said that travelers on the dangerous trek would sometimes stop at Mills' home to recuperate. The mansion's wooden staircase, the tallest in New Mexico, was often bathed in devilish light from the over 100-year-old "ruby" window set in the transom over the front door. Tragically, the window was recently stolen.

Mills was already a member of the infamous Santa Fe Ring and thus a major player in the vicious Colfax County War. He made many enemies in northern New Mexico in the 1870s as he worked to evict settlers, some of whom had lived on

For over a century a "ruby" transom window cast a forbidding light on the tallest wooden staircase in New Mexico.

"their" land for decades. These evictions were at the behest of the English and later Dutch companies that purchased the 1,714,765-acre (and by then wildly contested) Maxwell Land Grant. Practicing this type of law in the Wild West was far from a clean business, and the colonel was occasionally associated with violence. He was implicated in the murder of Methodist preacher and Ring opponent Franklin J. Tolby, and while the charge was quickly retracted, Mills's accuser, Manuel Cardenas, was himself shot on his way from court by an unknown assailant. Mills stated that he had been in Colorado on business when Cardenas was killed and was taken into protective custody with another Ring member. A third Ring affiliate had earlier lit out for Santa Fe with the hot-headed (and by then vehemently anti-Santa Fe Ring) Clay Allison's posse at his heels. In the interest of fairness, Mills trial was moved to Taos where a grand jury dropped all charges.

Dark political intrigue and bloodshed aside, Mills had a way with fruits and nuts and his Orchard Ranch, sprawled within a lush canyon of the Canadian River, became renowned, at one point containing 14,000 trees. In addition, he raised cattle and grew vegetables. A stage line stopped at the front door of his Mills Canyon Hotel. Mills's beef and produce was shipped all over the U.S., and it is no coincidence that Springer was already a busy railroad town on the Santa Fe's line.

In 1904, heavy rains came and the swollen Canadian washed away Mills's agricultural empire entirely, leaving him a ruined man. He left the area but is supposed to have returned at the end of his life, asking his former Santa Fe Ring partner, Thomas B.

The south side of the Mills Mansion, complete with massive cistern.

Catron, if he could die on a cot in the beautiful house that man now owned. However, Catron had died over four years earlier, in the spring of 1921, raising questions as to how he gave his consent. In fact, there is no evidence Catron even owned the mansion, although he bought some of the original Maxwell Land Grant from Mills. Somewhat more likely is that the president of the bank in Springer, who did own the home and was a friend and neighbor, granted the request, but I wonder if this is true; the August 21, 1925, edition of the *The Springer Times* makes no mention of any of it when announcing Mills' death, only saying he "passed away at his home in Springer." Mills certainly died on August 19, 1925, age seventy-nine. The next day, he had been scheduled to give a talk at the New Mexico Historical Society. While virtually nothing remains of his once-vast holdings, a small community to the southeast still bears his name.

Might Melvin Whitson Mills still reside in his mansion? There are many sources that say he does. Yet when I asked a former owner during my visit, all I received was a smile and the cryptic reply: "I don't know what you're talking about."

So raise a glass to the ghosts that are known to exist and those that may not. May both live on into eternity, telling us of their hopes and dreams, their loves and sorrows, their successes and failures. They have much to say, if only now and then we can become as still as they are and listen closely. Then we, too, will know exactly what they are talking about.

BIBLIOGRAPHY

"Arrive in El Paso: Lee and Gilliland on Way to Alamogordo Jail," *The Albuquerque Daily Citizen*, June 4, 1899.

"Fire wipes out Ricardo," *Santa Fe New Mexican,* May 8, 1908.

"Nation: What Happened to Our Men?" *Time Magazine.* Feb. 18, 1980, content.time.com/time/magazine/article/0,9171,921818-1,00.html

afflictor.com/tag/black-jack-ketchum/

American Newspaper Directory (New York: Geo. P. Rowell & Co., 1891)

Ayer, N. W. and Son. *N.W. Ayer & Son's American Newspaper Annual* (Philadelphia: N.W. Ayer & Son. 1884)

bestplaces.net/people/zip-code/new_mexico/monticello/87939

biography.com/people/conrad-hilton-9339383#

blm.gov/visit/lake-valley-historic-townsite

Boyle, D., *A History of Highway 60 and the Railroad Towns on the Belen, New Mexico Cutoff* (Santa Fe: Sunstone Press. 2015); *Highway 60 & the Belen Cutoff: A Brief History* (Denver. Outskirts Press. 2010)

Bryan, S. M., "NM's historic Fort Bayard up for sale," *Albuquerque Journal*, Feb. 2, 2014, abqjournal.com/346485/nms-historic-fort-bayard-up-for-sale.html

Burroughs, J. M. [ed.], *Roosevelt County History and Heritage* (Portales, 1975)

cabq.gov/council/projects/completed-projects/2014/albuquerque-rail-yards-redevelopment

Caffey, D. L., *Frank Springer and New Mexico: From the Colfax County War to the Emergence of Modern Santa Fe* (College Station: Texas A & M Press, 2006)

centerofthewest.org/explore/buffalo-bill/research/annie-oakley/

cityofdust.blogspot.com/2015/08/too-small-to-be-village-not-large.html

cityofdust.blogspot.com/2016/04/little-place-on-prairie-dunlap-new.html

cityofdust.blogspot.com/2016/05/the-ruins-by-rails-ricardo-new-mexico.html

cityofdust.blogspot.com/2017/10/nasario-remembers-rio-puerco.html

Colvin, M., "The New Mexico Prison Riot: Answers to Your Questions by Professor Colvin," radford.edu/~junnever/colvin.htm

"Cops: Interstate 40 a River of Crime," *KRQE News*, April 30, 2013. youtube.com/watch?v=uNH7c_9PAGM

debaca.nmgenweb.us/resources/other_places/taiban.html

Department of Interior, *Census Bulletin #37: Population of New Mexico by Countries and Minor Civil Divisions* (Washington, D.C.: Census Office, 1901)

Department of Interior, *Census Bulletin #129: Population of New Mexico by Minor Civil Divisions* (Washington, D.C.: Census Office, 1901)

elchuqueno.com/city-of-dust-center-point-new-mexico/

en.wikipedia.org/wiki/Buffalo_Soldier_tragedy_of_1877

en.wikipedia.org/wiki/Causey,_New_Mexico

en.wikipedia.org/wiki/Encino,_New_Mexico

en.wikipedia.org/wiki/Goodnight%E2%80%93Loving_Trail

en.wikipedia.org/wiki/Jornada_del_Muerto

en.wikipedia.org/wiki/Melvin_Whitson_Mills

en.wikipedia.org/wiki/Mescalero_Ridge

en.wikipedia.org/wiki/Organ,_New_Mexico

en.wikipedia.org/wiki/St._James_Hotel_(Cimarron,_New_Mexico)

en.wikipedia.org/wiki/Tom_Ketchum

en.wikipedia.org/wiki/Vaughn,_New_Mexico

en.wikipedia.org/wiki/Victorio

facebook.com/cityofdustnm

facebook.com/fortbayardhistoricpreservationsociety

facebook.com/Steins-NM-Railroad-Ghost-Town-111434342314414/

Garcia, N., *Hoe, Heaven, and Hell: My Boyhood in Rural New Mexico* (Albuquerque: University of New Mexico Press, 2015)

gendisasters.com/new-mexico/9313/carthage-nm-mine-explosion-dec-1907

Geronimo Trail National Scenic Byway/Sierra County Recreation & Tourism Advisory Board. *Historic Chloride: A Guide to a Classic, Old West Ghost Town.*

ghosttowns.com/states/nm/carthage.html

ghosttowns.com/states/nm/chloride.html

ghosttowns.com/states/nm/duran.html

ghosttowns.com/states/nm/engle.html

ghosttowns.com/states/nm/monticello.html

ghosttowns.com/states/nm/montoya.html

ghosttowns.com/states/nm/organ.html

ghosttowns.com/states/nm/sanpedro-socorro.html

ghosttowns.com/states/nm/steins.html

ghosttowns.com/states/nm/yeso.html

Gilbreath, W. C., *Death on the Gallows: The Story of Legal Hangings in New Mexico, 1847–1923* (Silver City: High-Lonesome Books, 2002)

Gliona, J. M. and Vaughn, N.M., "Police force goes to the dog. Really," *The Los Angeles Times,* Sept. 28, 2012, articles.latimes.com/2012/sep/28/nation/la-na-nn-new-mexico-police-dog-20120928

Harris, L. G., *Ghost Towns Alive: Trips to New Mexico's Past* (Albuquerque: University of New Mexico Press, 2003)

Herman, B., *Mountainair, N.M., Centennial History, 1903–2003* (Mountainair: Mountainair Public Schools, 2003)

Hildebrand, G., *Designing for Industry; the Architecture of Albert Ahn* (Cambridge: MIT Press, 1974)

Historic Preservation Division, *Application for Registration: New Mexico State Register of Cultural Properties* (Santa Fe, 2009), nmhistoricpreservation.org/documents/cprc/TaibanChurch.pdf

Historical Society of New Mexico, *New Mexico Historical Review, Vol. 1* (Santa Fe: Museum Press, 1926)

historynet.com/warm-springs-apache-leader-nana-the-80-year-old-warrior-turned-the-tables.htm

Hoffman, G. K. and Hereford, J. P., "Mining history of the Carthage coal field, Socorro County, New Mexico," in Lueth, V., Lucas, S. G., and Chamberlin, R. M. [eds.], *Geology of the Chupadera Mesa* (New Mexico Geological Society 60th Annual Fall Field Conference Guidebook), 438 p., nmgs.nmt.edu/publications/guidebooks/downloads/60/60_p0407_p0414.pdf

Julyan, R., *The Place Names of New Mexico: Revised Edition* (Albuquerque: University of New Mexico Press, 1998)

Lake, S. N., *Wyatt Earp: Frontier Marshall* (New York City: Houghton Mifflin Harcourt, 1931)

legendsofamerica.com/nm-etown/

legendsofamerica.com/nm-ghostwesttucumcari/

legendsofamerica.com/nm-placita/

legendsofamerica.com/we-blackjackketchum/

Looney, R., *Haunted Highways: The Ghost Towns of New Mexico* (Albuquerque: University of New Mexico Press, 1979)

"M. W. Mills is Dead," *The Springer Times,* August 21, 1925.

McDevitt, K. and Sitzberger, E., *History of the St. James Hotel: Cimarron, New Mexico* (Colorado Springs: Cimarron Press, 2019)

McKenna, J. A., *Black Range Tales* (Silver City: High-Lonesome Books, 2006)

McLaughlin, K., "A ghost town, dressing in vinegar," *Wall Street Journal*, June 6, 2013, wsj.com/articles/SB10001424127887323975004578499360574856572

Montoya, M. E., *Translating Property: The Maxwell Land Grant and the Conflict over Land in the American West, 1840–1900* (Berkeley, Los Angeles and London: University of California Press, 2002)

Morris, R., *The Devil's Butcher Shop: The New Mexico Prison Uprising* (Albuquerque: University of New Mexico Press, 1988)

newmexicohistory.org/places/fort-bayard nmfarmandranchmuseum.org/oralhistory/detail.php?interview=144

newmexiconomad.com/lake-valley-new-mexico/

Palmer, R. Q., "City marshal, Pete Barker, killed," *Clayton Citizen*, August 6, 1909.

Pearce, T. M., *New Mexico Place Names: A Geographical Dictionary* (Albuquerque: University of New Mexico Press, 1983)

Pike, D. and Pike, A., *Detour New Mexico: Historic Destinations and Natural Wonders* (Charleston: The History Press, 2017)

Pike, D., "The Mills Mansion: found and lost," *New Mexico Magazine*, October 2015, newmexico.org/nmmagazine/articles/post/found-lost-93375/

Pike, D., *Roadside New Mexico: A Guide to Historic Markers-Revised and Expanded Edition* (Albuquerque: University of New Mexico Press, 2015)

pioneerstoremuseum.com/

Plant, G. "Preservation group backing plan for Fort Bayard," *Silver City Daily Press*, Feb. 8, 2019, scdailypress.com/site/2019/02/08/preservation-group-backing-plan-for-fort-bayard/

Poling-Kempes, L., *The Harvey Girls: Women Who Opened the West* (New York: Marlowe & Company, 1989)

prorodeohalloffame.com/inductees/by-category/tie-down-roping/glen-franklin/

Ramirez, F., *Remembering Fierro (Again): Revised Edition* (Self-published)

route66news.com/2011/12/11/elderly-woman-may-be-new-owner-of-old-cuervo-school/

Salt of the Earth, Dir. Biberman, H. J., 1954. youtube.com/watch?v=5Dt2PKU4yLg

santafetrailnm.org/site537.html

Schafersman, S. *Introduction to the Llano Estacado*, llanoestacado.org/resources/llano_estacado.pdf

Schedules of the New Mexico Territory Census, 1885, NARA Microfilm Publication M846, 6 rolls. Record of the Bureau of the Census, Record Group 29. Washington, D.C.: National Archives.

Sherman, J. E. and Sherman, B. H., *Ghost Towns and Mining Camps of New Mexico* (Norman: University of Oklahoma Press, 1975)

sierracountynewmexico.info/attractions/percha-bank-museum-kingston/

spaceportamerica.com/

Springer, C., "Kingston's myth of 7,000 souls: was the mining boomtown really once the biggest town in New Mexico Territory?" *Desert Exposure*, 2012, desertexposure.com/201206/201206_kingston_myth.php

Stanley, F., *The Causey (New Mexico) Story* (Pep, 1966)

staythirstymedia.com/201211-075/html/201211-wolf-duran.html

texasescapes.com/TexasPanhandleTowns/Pep-Texas.htm

theroadwanderer.net/66NMex/montoya.htm

theroadwanderer.net/66NMex/newkirk.htm

Torrance County Historical Society, *History of Torrance County* (Torrance County: Torrance County Historical Society, 1979)

Tórrez, R. J., *Myth of the Hanging Tree: Stories of Crime and Punishment in Territorial New Mexico* (Albuquerque: University of New Mexico Press, 2008)

tshaonline.org/handbook/online/articles/fca98

Varney, P., *New Mexico's Best Ghost Towns: A Practical Guide* (Albuquerque: University of New Mexico Press, 1981)

wheelsmuseum.org

Whitlock, V. H., *Cowboy Life on the Llano Estacado* (Norman: University of Oklahoma Press, 1970)

Williams, E. C., *Chaves County Schools 1881–1968: Treasures of New Mexico History* (Roswell, 2000)

INDEX

San Augustin Peak 122, 124
San Carlos Reservation 115
San Francisco Chronicle 145
San Ignacio Catholic Church 117
San Jose Catholic Church 21-22
San Juan Bautista Catholic Church 33
San Juan Pueblo 11
San Marcial (Village of) 15, 38
San Pedro (Village of) 39-40
San Pedro Catholic Church 39
San Pedro Cemetery 40
San Ysidro (Village of) 17
Santa Rita Church 20
Santa Rita (County of Socorro) (see Riley)
Santa Rita (County of Grant) 108
Santa Fe (City of) 78, 103, 128, 148
Santa Fe (County of) 39
Santa Fe New Mexican 52, 144
Santa Fe Prison Riot 128-132
Santa Fe Railroad (SF) 35-36, 41
Santa Fe Ring 147-149
Santa Fe Territorial Prison 144
Santa Fe Trail (Mountain/Cimarron Route) 140-141, 147
Santa Maria, Zeke P. 114
Santa Rita (Village of) 19-20
Savannah River 10
Seville (City of, Spain) 21
Shakespeare, William 146
Shamrock Gas Station 82
Sheddon, Jack 94
Sherman, Barbara H. 38
Sherman, James E. 38
Shields, Otis L. 63
Sierra (County of) 92, 117
Sierra Grande Mining Company 97
Silver City (City of) 86, 90, 97, 101, 105, 108
Sinclair Gas Station 84
Slumbering Mountain Cemetery 123
Smith, Ed 28
Smith, Mac 64
Socorro (County of) 21, 35, 39
Socorro (Town of) 39, 119
Solitaire Mine 94
South, The 27
South Carolina (State of) 9-10
Southern Apache Agency 115
Southern Pacific Railroad 84, 124, 126
Southwest, The 96
Spaceport America 121
Spain (Country of) 21, 118
Spanish (Language) 41, 45, 47, 54, 72, 107, 138
Spanish Empire 11
Springer (Town of) 49, 146-149
Springer, Frank 147

Springer Times 149
Spurs Saloon 50
Staked Plain (see Llano Estacado)
Stanley, F. 66, 67
Steens, Enoch 124
Steins (Village of) 124-127
Steins Pass 124, 144
Steins Peak 124, 126
Steins Peak Station 124
Stephens, William Jack 131
Stinson Cattle Trail 50
Stinson, Jim 50
Stitzel, Dave 90
Sullivan, John 117
Super Service Drive In 54-55
Sunshine Grocery 75

Tafoya, Jose 19
Tafoya, Luis 19
Taiban (Village of) 56-59, 74
Taiban Creek 56
Taiban International Airport 58
Taiban Savings Bank 56
Taiban Spring 56
Taiban Trading Post 57
Taos (City of) 134, 138, 148
Taylor, William 28
Tefoya family 39
Tennessee (State of) 10
Tenorio 45
Terminator Salvation 15
Terry, Meryl 70
Texas (State of) 24, 33, 50, 54, 56, 58, 65, 68, 70, 74, 76, 84, 100, 138, 141-142, 145
Then We'll be Happy 27
Thornton, Reverend S. W. 94
Thornton, William 147
Tolby, Franklin J. 148
Tombstone Epitaph 94
Torrance County Board of Education 28
Torrance County Singing Convention 25, 27
Torrez, Robert J. 32
Tres Hermanos Mine (Carthage) 37
Trinidad (City of, Colorado) 144
Trinity Test Site 11, 27-28, 39
Truth or Consequences (City of) 86, 92-93, 115, 118
Tuberculosis 52, 105
Tucumcari (City of) 74, 78, 85
Tularosa Basin 122
Tularosa Basin Downwinders Consortium 28
Turner, Ted 121

U & I Bar 48
Union Army 97